THE ANCIENT ROMAN WORLD

ΣΑΜΙΟΣ ΕΠΟΙΗΣΕ

RONALD MELLOR &
AMANDA H. PODANY
GENERAL EDITORS

THE ANCIENT ROMAN WORLD

Ronald Mellor & Marni McGee

Lovingly dedicated to Anne Mellor and Sears McGee—
fine scholars and our best friends.

OXFORD
UNIVERSITY PRESS

Oxford New York
Auckland Bangkok Buenos Aires Cape Town Chennai Dar es Salaam Delhi Hong Kong Istanbul Karachi Kolkata Kuala Lumpur Madrid Melbourne Mexico City Mumbai Nairobi São Paulo Shanghai Singapore Taipei Tokyo Toronto

Published by Oxford University Press, Inc.
198 Madison Avenue, New York, New York 10016
www.oup.com

Library of Congress Cataloging-in-Publication Data

Mellor, Ronald.
The ancient Roman world / Ronald Mellor & Marni McGee.
p. cm. — (The world in ancient times)
Summary: Introduces the history, culture, and people of ancient Rome
and examines its many contributions to the development of Western society.
Includes bibliographical references and index.
ISBN-13: 978-0-19-515380-4 ISBN-10: 0-19-515380-4
ISBN-13: 978-0-19-522249-4 (California edition) ISBN-10: 0-19-522249-0 (California edition)
ISBN-13: 978-0-19-522242-5 (set) ISBN-10: 0-19-522242-3 (set)
1. Rome—History—Kings, 753-510 B.C.—Juvenile literature.
2. Rome—History—Republic, 510-30 B.C.—Juvenile literature.
3. Rome—History—Empire, 30 B.C.-284 A.D.—Juvenile literature.
[1. Rome—History. 2. Rome—Civilization.] I. McGee, Marni. II. Title.
III. Series.
DG231 .M45 2004
937—dc22 2003017799

9 8 7 6 5 4 3 2 1

Printed in the United States of America on acid-free paper

Design: Stephanie Blumenthal
Layout: Lenny Levitsky
Cover design and logo: Nora Wertz

On the cover: A child rides in a horse-drawn cart from a relief from a child's sarcophagus.
Frontispiece: Musicians perform in a street scene in a mosaic from Cicero's villa in Pompeii.

RONALD MELLOR &
AMANDA H. PODANY
GENERAL EDITORS

DIANE L. BROOKS, ED.D.
EDUCATION CONSULTANT

The Early Human World
Peter Robertshaw & Jill Rubalcaba

The Ancient Near Eastern World
Amanda H. Podany & Marni McGee

The Ancient Egyptian World
Eric H. Cline & Jill Rubalcaba

The Ancient South Asian World
Jonathan Mark Kenoyer & Kimberley Heuston

The Ancient Chinese World
Terry Kleeman & Tracy Barrett

The Ancient Greek World
Jennifer T. Roberts & Tracy Barrett

The Ancient Roman World
Ronald Mellor & Marni McGee

The Ancient American World
William Fash & Mary E. Lyons

The World in Ancient Times: Primary Sources and Reference Volume
Ronald Mellor & Amanda H. Podany

CONTENTS

A [“] marks each chapter's main primary sources—ancient writings and artifacts that "speak" to us from the past.

CAST OF CHARACTERS

Because The World in Ancient Times *covers many cultures, we use the abbreviations* CE *for "Common Era" and* BCE *for "Before the Common Era." The traditional equivalents are* BC *for "Before Christ" and* AD *for* "Anno Domini," *Latin for "In the Year of Our Lord," referring to the birth of Jesus Christ.*

Aeneas (ay-NEE-us) Legendary prince, son of goddess Venus in Plutarch's telling of the founding of Rome

Agrippa (uh-GRIP-uh), about 63–12 BCE Roman general, ally of Augustus Caesar; Agrippa married Augustus's daughter, Julia

Agrippa (uh-GRIP-uh) **Menenius** (men-EN-ee-us) Roman leader who ended a workers' rebellion by telling the fable of the belly

Agrippina (AG-ri-PEE-nuh), 15–59 CE Great-granddaughter of Augustus; married to Emperor Claudius I, whom she poisoned so that her son, Nero, would become emperor

Alexander the Great, 356–323 BCE King of Macedon (336–323 BCE); conquered Egypt and parts of Asia

Antiochus III (an-TIE-uh-kus), 242–187 BCE King of western Asia (223–187 BCE); invaded Greece and was defeated by the Roman army

Appian (AP-ee-un), 2nd century CE Roman historian born in Greece; wrote *Civil Wars*

Arminius (ar-MIN-ee-us), d. 19 CE German chief who defeated Varus in 9 CE

Augustus (aw-GUS-tus) **Caesar** (SEE-zer), also Octavian, 63 BCE–14 CE First Roman emperor and heir of Julius Caesar; ruled as Augustus (27 BCE–14 CE)

Brutus (BROO-tus), about 85–42 BCE A protégé of Julius Caesar; became one of Caesar's assassins

Caesar (SEE-zer), **Julius**, about 100–44 BCE Roman statesman and general, named Roman dictator (48–44 BCE); conspirators murdered him in Senate House

Caesarion (see-ZAIR-ee-un), 47–30 BCE Cleopatra's son by Julius Caesar

Caligula (kuh-LIG-yu-luh), 12–41 CE Succeeded Tiberius as emperor (37–41 CE); was known for cruelty and ruthlessness

Caracalla (kah-rah-KAH-luh), 188–217 CE Succeeded his father, Severus, as Roman emperor (212–217 CE)

Cassius (KASS-ee-us) **Dio** (DIE-o), about 155–235 CE Roman historian

Cato (KAY-toh), **Marcus Porcius** (POR-shee-us), or Cato the Censor, 234–148 BCE Roman statesman and moralist

Cicero (SIS-uh-ro), **Marcus Tullius** (TOOL-ee-us), 106–43 BCE Roman statesman, orator, and philosopher

Cincinnatus (SIN-suh-nah-tus), 5th century BCE Farmer and patriot; served twice as dictator (458 and 439 BCE)

Claudius (KLAW-dee-us), 10 BCE–54 CE Succeeded Caligula as emperor (41–54 CE)

Cleopatra VII, 69–30 BCE Queen of Egypt (51–30 BCE); last of the Ptolemaic dynasty

Constantine the Great, 272–337 CE Roman emperor (306–337 CE)

Crassus (KRASS-us), about 115–53 BCE Roman general; suppressed slave revolt of 73 BCE; formed First Triumvirate with Julius Caesar and Pompey

Diocletian, about 243–312 CE Roman emperor (284–305 CE)

Diodorus (DIE-uh-DOR-us), 1st century BCE Greek historian; wrote 40 books of world history

Dionysius (DIE-un-ISH-ee-us) **of Halicarnassus** (HAL-i-kar-NA-sus), late 1st century BCE Greek historian; longest work is *Roman Antiquities*

Domitian (duh-MISH-un), 51–96 CE Son of Vespasian; Roman emperor (81–96 CE)

Gracchi (GRAK-eye) The brothers Tiberius (about 164–133 BCE) and Gaius Gracchus (about 153–121 BCE); Roman statesmen and social reformers

Hadrian (HAY-dree-un), 76–138 CE Roman emperor (117–138 CE)

Hamilcar (HAM-ul-kar) **Barca** (BAR-kuh), d. 229 BCE Carthaginian general who fought in First Punic War against Rome; father of Hannibal

Hannibal, 247–183 or 182 BCE Carthaginian general who fought in Second Punic War against Rome

Herod, 73–4 BCE King of Judea (40–4 BCE)

Herodotus (huh-RAH-duh-tus), about 485–425 BCE Greek historian; "Father of History"

Horace (HOR-iss), 65–8 BCE Latin lyric poet

Horatius (huh-RAY-shee-us) 5th century BCE Legendary Roman hero who stood ground against Etruscans' attack on Rome in 475 BCE

Jesus of Nazareth 4 BCE–29 CE Proclaimed Messiah (Christ) by followers

Josephus (jo-SEE-fus), about 37–100 CE Jewish historian

Judas Maccabeus (mak-kah-BEE-us) d. 160 BCE Leader of Jewish revolt against king of Syria

Julia Domna, 3rd century CE Roman empress; wife to Emperor Severus; mother of Emperor Caracalla

Justinian, 482–565 CE Roman emperor at Constantinople (527–565 CE)

Juvenal (JOO-vuh-null), 2nd century CE Roman satirical poet

Lepidus (LEP-i-dus), 90–12 BCE Joined with Octavian and Antony in Second Triumvirate

Livia, 55 BCE–29 CE First Roman empress; wife of Augustus Caesar; mother of the emperor Tiberius

Livy, 59 BCE–17 CE Roman historian; wrote *From the Founding of the City*

Lucretia (loo-KREE-shuh) Roman legendary figure known for her virtue; Sextus's attack on her ended the reign of Tarquin the Proud

Marcus Aurelius (MAR-kus ow-REL-ee-us), 121–180 CE Roman emperor (161–180 CE) and philosopher

Mark Antony, about 83–30 BCE Roman politician and soldier; married Cleopatra in 36 BCE

Martial (MAR-shul), about 40–104 CE Spanish poet; lived in Rome after 64 CE

Nero (NEAR-o), 37–68 CE Roman emperor (54–68 CE)

Nerva (NERV-uh), 30–98 CE Chosen by Senate to be Roman emperor (96–98 CE); chose Trajan as his successor

Octavia (ahk-TAY-vee-ah), d. 11 BCE Sister of Augustus; wife of Mark Antony

Octavian, or **Octavius**. *See* **Augustus Caesar**

Paul of Tarsus, d. about 64 CE
Preached the Christian religion to non-Jews

Pliny (PLIH-nee) **the Elder**, about 23–79 CE
Roman scientist; wrote encyclopedia of natural science; died while observing the eruption of Mt. Vesuvius

Pliny (PLIH-nee) **the Younger**, about 62–113 CE
Roman orator and statesman; nephew of Pliny the Elder

Plutarch (PLOO-tark), 46–120 CE
Greek philosopher and biographer

Polybius (puh-LIB-ee-us), 203–120 BCE   Greek historian

Pompey (PAHM-pee), 106–48 CE
Roman general, rival of Julius Caesar

Ptolemy I (TALL-uh-mee), about 367–282 BCE   General under Alexander the Great; King of Egypt (305–282 BCE), the first of the Ptolemaic dynasty

Ptolemy XIII (TALL-uh-mee), 63–47 BCE   King of Egypt (51–47 BCE), co-ruled with his sister Cleopatra until she had him killed

Romulus (ROM-yuh-lus)
Founder of Rome in legend recounted by Livy

Sallust (SAL-ust), about 86–35 BCE
Roman historian and senator; served with Julius Caesar

Scipio Africanus (SIP-ee-o af-ri-KAH-nus), 236–183 BCE
Roman general; defeated Hannibal at Zama in 202 BCE

Seneca (SEN-i-kuh), about 3 BCE–65 CE
Roman statesman and philosopher

Severus (suh-VEER-us), **Septimius** (sep-TIM-ee-us), 146–211 CE
Roman emperor (193–211 CE)

Spartacus (SPAR-tuh-kus), d. 71 BCE   Slave and gladiator; led slave revolt in 73 BCE

Suetonius (swee-TOE-nee-us), 69–140 CE   Roman biographer; wrote *Lives of the Twelve Caesars*

Tacitus (TASS-i-tus), about 55–117 CE   Roman historian and biographer

Tarquin (TAR-kwin) **the Proud**, d. 495 BCE   Rome's seventh and last king (534–510 BCE)

Tarquinius (tar-KWIN-ee-us) **Sextus**, 6th century BCE
Legendary prince whose attack on Lucretia led to the downfall of his father, Tarquin the Proud

Theodosius, 346–395 CE   Roman emperor (379–395 CE)

Tiberius (tie-BEER-ee-us), 42 BCE–37 CE   Second Roman emperor (14–37 CE)

Titus (TIE-tus), 39–81 CE
Succeeded his father, Vespasian, as Roman emperor (79–81 CE)

Trajan (TRAY-jun), 53–117 CE
Selected by Nerva to be his successor as Roman emperor (98–117 CE)

Varus, d. 9 CE   Roman general who lost three legions in Germany

Vespasian (vuh-SPAY-zhun), 9–79 CE   Roman military leader; emperor (69–79 CE)

Vestal (VES-tul) **Virgins**   Unmarried female priestesses who performed sacred rituals honoring the goddess Vesta

Virgil (VER-jul), 70–19 BCE
Roman poet; wrote epic *Aeneid*

Tyne River
York
North Sea
Baltic Sea
BRITAIN
Londinium
Rhine River
GERMANY
Bonn
Lutetia
(Paris)
Atlantic Ocean
GAUL
(FRANCE)
Danube River
Rhône River
ILLYRIA
Alps
Pisa
Marseilles
ITALY
Adriatic Sea
Rome
Cannae
Capua
Naples
Pompeii
SPAIN
Saguntum
Actium
Mycenae
Misenum
Sicily
Syracuse
Carthage
Zama
Mediterranean Sea
AFRICA

SOME PRONUNCIATIONS

Actium (AK-tee-um)
Antioch (ANN-tee-ahk)
Cannae (KAN-nay)
Capua (KAP-oo-uh)
Carthage (CAR-thij)
Dacia (DAY-shi-ah)
Damascus (duh-MASS-kus)
Ephesus (EF-ah-sus)
Illyria (i-LEER-ee-uh)
Lutetia (loo-TAY-see-uh)
Lydia (LIH-dee-uh)
Marseilles (mar-SAY)
Masada (muh-SAHD-uh)
Misenum (my-SEE-num)
Mycenae (my-SEE-nee)
Naples (NAY-puhls)
Nazareth (NAZ-uh-ruhth)
Phoenicia (Fi-NISH-uh)
Pisa (PEE-suh)
Pompeii (pahm-PAY)
Saguntum (sah-GUN-tum)
Sicily (SIS-uh-lee)
Syracuse (SEER-uh-kyoose)
Syria (SEER-ee-uh)
Tarsus (TAR-sus)
Zama (ZAH-muh)

CHAPTER 1

VIRGIL, DIONYSIUS, AND LIVY

WIVES, WOLVES, AND WILD BOYS

THE FOUNDING OF ROME

Virgil, *The Aeneid,* 19 BCE

I sing of war and of that man who first came in exile from the shores of Troy to the coast of Italy. He was battered on land and sea by divine violence, . . . He had to suffer much in war until he built a city. . . . From him came the Latin people, . . . and the high walls of Rome.

With his homeland in enemy hands and his city in flames, Prince Aeneas, son of the goddess Venus, led a small

The Roman wolf is feeding the two abandoned babies, Romulus and Remus, who founded Rome. This bronze sculpture, made about 500 BCE, is still a symbol of Rome.

group of Trojans to sea. After many months of being tossed about by fierce winds and storms, the travelers finally anchored their ships near the mouth of the Tiber River in Italy. Yet no sooner had they landed than the men began to plan another voyage.

This appalled the Trojan women. As the Greek historian Dionysius records the story, a noblewoman named Roma secretly took the women aside and suggested that they take matters into their own hands. "Tired of wandering," the others listened eagerly. "Roma stirred up the . . . Trojan women" and suggested a simple plan. They all agreed, and "together, they set fire to the ships."

Dionysius, *Roman Antiquities*, 8 BCE

At first the men were furious, but pretty soon they realized that the women had done the right thing. They had landed in a perfect spot. With mild weather and beautiful countryside—a cluster of hills just 15 miles from the sea—why should they leave? The men were so pleased that they named the place after Roma, the rebellious wife.

The Roman historian Livy had also written down a different legend about two brothers who were sons of the king. Their names were Numitor and Amulius. When their father the king died, Amulius grabbed the throne and forced Numitor to leave the kingdom. But then Amulius worried that someone might try to overthrow *him*. What if Numitor's daughter, Rhea Silvia, had children who might try to take the throne? Amulius wasn't taking any chances. He forced Rhea Silvia to join the Vestal Virgins—a group of women who served in the temple of the goddess Vesta. The Romans believed that Vesta wanted the complete attention of her priestesses, so the Vestal Virgins were not allowed to marry or have children.

Poor Rhea had no choice but to obey her uncle. But things didn't go according to Amulius's plan. Somehow, despite her protected life among the Vestal Virgins, Rhea became pregnant and gave birth to twins—two strong, handsome boys. She named her sons Romulus and Remus. Amulius was outraged when he heard the news. He ordered his servants to take the twins from their mother's arms and drown them in the river. Rhea herself was bound and thrown into prison.

THE FOUNDING OF A CITY

A city's founding is the time when the first settlers pitch their tents or build buildings and start to call it "home." The founder of a city or country is the person who makes that happen. Because Rome was founded and named in prehistoric times, we depend in part on legends to piece together its history.

A Greek poet named Homer composed the story of the Trojan War. For centuries, people thought he had made up an imaginary city and its people, the Trojans. Then in 1870, an amateur archaeologist, Heinrich Schliemann, astonished the scholars: he found the buried remains of Troy. The ancient city was real after all.

The servant couldn't bring himself to kill the babies, so he put them into a basket and set it afloat on the river. He was sure that the babies would be carried away and drowned as the king had commanded. But the river was kind and gently landed the basket on solid ground.

Although the twins didn't drown, they were still in great danger. If they didn't starve, wild animals might eat them. Miraculously, according to Livy, "a she-wolf, coming down from the . . . hills to quench her thirst, turned her steps towards the cry of the infants, and nursed them so gently that the keeper of the royal flock found her licking them with her tongue."

Livy, *From the Founding of the City*, 25 BCE

When the herdsman found Romulus and Remus, he took them home. He and his wife raised the boys as their own. The twins grew to be brave, manly, and noble. They roamed the countryside like ancient Robin Hoods, often saving innocent people from danger and persecution.

MEANWHILE IN SOUTH ASIA . . .

In ancient societies there are many stories of unwanted children who were abandoned in baskets and set adrift on a river. The Indian god Krishna, the Mesopotamian king Sargon, and the Hebrew lawgiver Moses all suffered the same fate as Romulus and Remus, and all of them survived.

Romulus and Remus eventually discovered who they really were and decided to found a new city near the Tiber River, where they had been rescued as babies. But the brothers didn't get along very well, and they disagreed about where the city should be built. They tried to settle their argument through divination, using the path of birds in the sky to figure out the wishes of the gods. They decided to watch some vultures flying overhead. Romulus tried to trick Remus, pretending to have spotted more vultures than he actually saw, and then Remus made fun of Romulus. The brothers got into a fight, and Romulus killed Remus.

Romulus buried his brother and then, with his followers, built a new city on the Palatine Hill and circled it with strong, stone walls. As the city grew, it eventually enclosed seven hills and took the name of its founder, Romulus—or Rome. The Romans dated everything that happened after that "from the founding of the city" in 753 BCE. For more than a thousand years, they used a calendar that began in that year.

Some Romans claimed that Romulus and Remus were the sons of Mars, the god of war. Later Romans believed that this connection to Mars explained Romulus's cruel

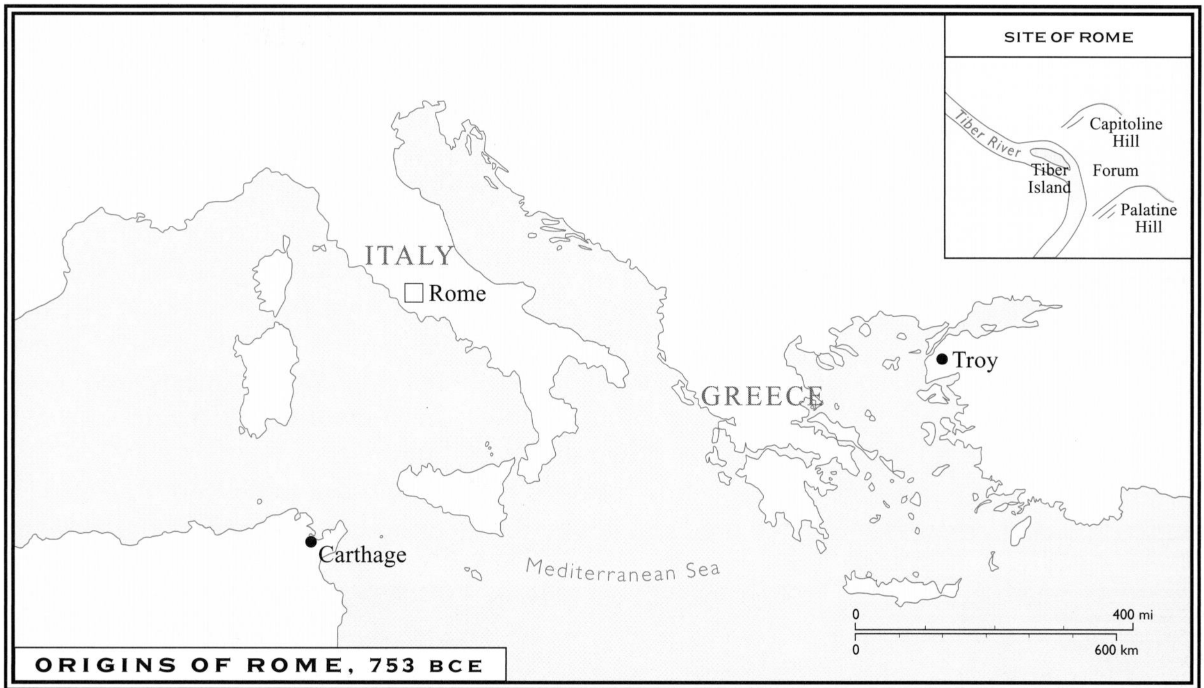

ORIGINS OF ROME, 753 BCE

attack on the Sabines, a tribe that lived in small, unprotected villages near Rome. Romulus was convinced that Rome would become great through war, so he pretended to invite his Sabine neighbors to a festival. But then he led the Romans in a sudden attack. The soldiers seized 30 unmarried women and ran off—taking the Sabine women home as their wives.

The reaction of the Sabine men is easy to guess: they set out to rescue the women. They attacked the walled city of Rome. A fierce battle between the Sabines and the Romans raged until a strange thing happened. Torn between love for their Sabine fathers and brothers and their love for the Romans who were now their husbands, the Sabine women ran onto the battleground. With desperate cries, hair tumbling to their shoulders, and infants in their arms, they begged the warriors on both sides to stop killing each other. Moved by the women's words and tears, the men called a truce, and the two peoples became one.

So what do we discover about the ancient Romans from these stories? For one thing, they believed that many gods were involved in their lives. Often a hero or leader, such as Aeneas, is believed to have had one mortal parent and one **immortal** one. This would explain why the gods cared so much about Rome, its beginnings, and its continued success.

mors = "death"
Ordinary human beings are mortal because they can die. Immortal beings—gods and goddesses—never die.

The first Roman histories give varying, sometimes contradictory, stories about the distant past—for example, the two very different legends about Rome's founding. That's because these tales began in prehistorical times, before people began writing down their histories. Storytellers passed the tales down orally for hundreds of years.

Family histories get passed down orally, too. And stories change and get better the more we tell them. Do members

In this 1633 painting, Romulus raises his cloak to signal the Romans to attack and seize the unsuspecting Sabine women.

of your family have different versions of events that happened only 20 or 30 years ago? Do you exaggerate a bit when you tell your friends about your adventures? In the same way, the myths and legends of Rome "improved" through thousands of tellings over hundreds of years. But these stories may carry a part of the truth.

Although myth and legend cloud the founding of Rome, archaeology shows that there is a trace of truth in these accounts. Latin-speaking herdsmen and small farmers did establish a settlement and build huts on the Palatine Hill in the 8th century BCE. These archaeological findings agree with the legendary foundation of Rome around 753.

As for the mingling of the Roman and Sabine peoples, cemeteries in Rome give evidence for that. Each early civilization followed a particular set of rules for burying its dead. But in Rome, archaeologists have found the remains of buried bodies and the ashes of cremated bodies—proof that two different cultures existed side-by-side in early Rome. This is one of many ways that archaeologists have found evidence of a real world that mirrors the ancient myths and legends of Rome.

Vesta's temples were always round; this one—in the Roman Forum—stands next to the house where the Vestal Virgins lived. Inside were the treasures that the Romans believed Aeneas brought from Troy.

WHAT YEAR BECOMES "YEAR ONE"?

In the year 46 BCE, the Roman leader Julius Caesar created the calendar we use today. But this was not the first calendar. Many other peoples had developed ways to keep track of time. The most important difference among them is the starting date.

The ancient Greek calendar began with the first Olympic Games in 776 BCE. The Hebrew calendar begins with the traditional date of Creation, when God created the world. And in the Muslim calendar, Year One is when the prophet Mohammed left the holy city of Mecca.

Christians used Caesar's calendar, but the starting point became the birth of Jesus, which is a bit like point zero on a thermometer. The years before his birth were called "BC" (Before Christ) and the years after his birth were "AD" (Anno Domini, Latin for "in the year of the Lord"). Today, most historians use BCE (Before the Common Era) instead of BC, and they have replaced AD with CE (Common Era).

CHAPTER 2

[66] HERODOTUS AND DIONYSIUS OF HALICARNASSUS

MIGRATION, MYSTERY, AND MASTERY

WHO WERE THE ETRUSCANS?

paene + *insula* = "almost" + "island" A peninsula like Italy is "almost an island" because it is surrounded on three sides by water.

The founders of Rome were not the first people to arrive on the Italian **peninsula.** For thousands of years before the city was born, settlers had been immigrating from all directions. Some came to escape war, as legend says the Trojans did. Others came seeking land and wealth. Some of the earliest settlers sailed from North Africa. Other tribes crossed the Alps to settle in Italy and its islands.

About 1000 BCE, Italic peoples arrived from across the Adriatic Sea. These immigrants brought new languages, one of which was Latin. The shepherds who first settled the Palatine Hill in the 8th century BCE spoke Latin, which became the official language of business and government in Rome. Latin gradually spread throughout the peninsula and eventually became the accepted language of the Roman empire.

PEOPLES OF ITALY, 500 BCE

The peninsula soon became home to other peoples as well: the Etruscans and the Greeks. Around 750 BCE, some cities in Greece set up colonies in southern Italy, especially on the island of Sicily. The cities wanted trading partners in other places so that they could buy and sell each other's goods. The Greek colonists who came to Italy were looking for land and the chance to make money through trade. They founded great cities like Naples, which has survived for 2,700 years and is still thriving today. The Greek colonists brought their art, architecture, literature, alphabet, and gods—all of which became a part of Roman culture.

The Etruscans settled north of Rome, at about the same time. We don't know where they came from, or why. Herodotus, a Greek historian of the fifth century BCE, believed that the Etruscans came from Lydia, part of the country we now call Turkey. He writes: "There was great

[66] Herodotus, *Histories*, 425 BCE

A young Etruscan musician, dressed in sandals and a knee-length robe, plays a double flute, joining other performers in an outdoor ceremony or festival.

poverty through the whole land of Lydia. . . . The king decided to divide the nation. . . . Half of the people would stay; the other half would leave. He would reign over those who stayed behind." The people who had to leave sailed to Umbria in northern Italy and built cities there. "They gave up their former name of Lydians and called themselves after the . . . king's son, who led the colony: Tyrrhenians."

Other ancient writers disagreed with Herodotus. Dionysius, a Greek who lived in Rome, writes in his history: "I do not believe . . . that the Tyrrhenians were a colony of Lydians; for they do not use the same language. . . . They don't worship the same gods as the Lydians or use the same laws and institutions."

“ Dionysius of Halicarnassus, *Roman Antiquities*, 8 BCE

Until recently, most historians thought that Herodotus was right. They believed that the Etruscans came as a united people from the east, bringing their language, religion, music, and dance. These scholars based their ideas on the evidence of Etruscan paintings. Images of music and dance in Etruscan artwork look a lot like images in Greek art. This led scholars to reason that the Etruscans must have come from a part of the Greek world or somewhere nearby.

But recent discoveries have begun to change their minds. Archaeologists have compared street patterns in many northern Italian towns and cities. They've studied how people in that region laid out their towns and cities and built their houses. Archaeologists realized that the Etruscan cities followed the same patterns as the earlier, much older towns further north. Because of these similarities, most historians now believe that the Etruscans, like Americans, didn't come as a group from any one place. Most now believe that the Etruscan culture took shape in northern Italy. The region was a melting pot where customs, skills, and beliefs of many different cultures combined to form the Etruscan civilization.

So what do we know for sure about the Etruscans? Archaeology tells us that these seafarers were already living in Italy by 900 BCE. They were brilliant architects—they invented the arch and the vault, which the Romans later used to build their enormous arenas. Etruscan artists and metalworkers made everything from iron plows to polished bronze mirrors, silver bowls, and elegant gold jewelry. They even made braces for teeth! And their sculptors created masterpieces in bronze and clay.

When most Italic peoples were still living in villages, the Etruscans had cities surrounded by strong, defensive walls, with elaborate temples inside. Each city elected its own officials, but when foreign armies

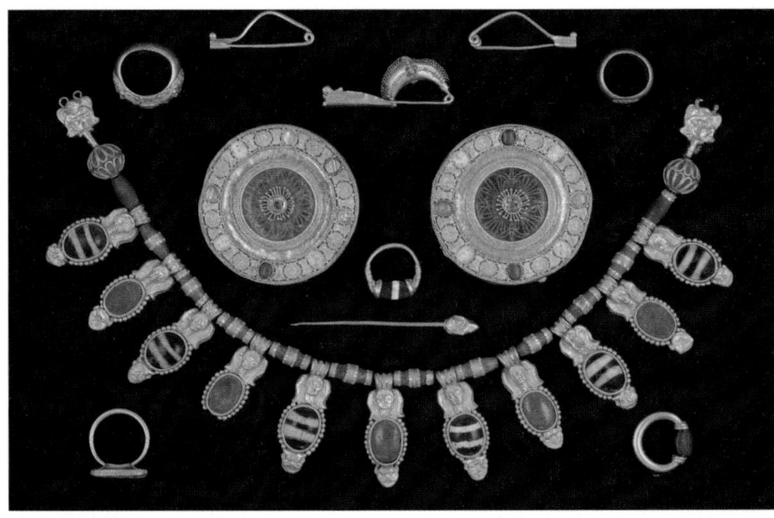

These necklaces, earrings, pins, and rings—crafted from gold, glass, and precious stones—once belonged to a very wealthy woman. An Etruscan artist created this jewelry in about 500 BCE.

threatened, the cities often joined forces and obeyed a single commander.

The Etruscans understood city planning, engineering, and waterworks much better than most other ancient peoples. And the Romans learned from them. The Etruscans' building skills helped Rome when it later laid out its own system of roads and waterways throughout its huge empire.

Imagine a marshy place where it's too wet to farm or graze sheep. How would you make a living there? Etruscan engineers solved this problem. They figured out how to drain land and make it useful. They dug interconnecting canals and built drains to carry extra water into the river or into reservoirs that held the city's water supply. When Etruscan kings ruled Rome, they drained a broad, marshy area and channeled the water into a huge drain called the Cloaca Maxima.

Once the land was drained, the Etruscans paved over it and built the Forum, Rome's marketplace and political center. This became the focus of community life in Rome. There, a person could buy bread or fish for dinner, hear a speech, meet friends, sell a slave, and check the sundial to find the time of day.

Most of our knowledge of the Etruscans' religious beliefs and daily life comes from their tombs. Some were large underground caverns the size of a room or even a house. Inside them, archaeologists have found pottery, furniture, small statues, and elaborate jewelry. The Etruscans believed in an afterlife and thought that after death people would still need clothes to wear and couches to rest on. They thought that the dead would still want to drink from painted pottery cups. When an Etruscan nobleman died, he might be buried with his hunting gear, his favorite vases and statues, even his chariot. His wife would be buried in the same tomb, dressed in her finest clothes and jewels so that the two could enjoy the afterlife together.

Perhaps the most useful discoveries in the tombs are the wall paintings. Through these paintings, the graves "talk" to us and give us a picture of everyday life. The paintings show men and women lounging side-by-side at a banquet.

ETRUSCAN RISE AND FALL

1000 BCE
Italic immigrants arrive in Italy

900 BCE
Etruscans appear in central Italy

750 BCE
Greeks establish colonies in southern Italy

616 BCE
Etruscans rule in Rome

509 BCE
Roman army defeats last Etruscan king

About 500 BCE
Greek cities defeat Etruscan army in south

266 BCE
Rome controls all Italy

An Etruscan husband and wife, sculpted in clay in the sixth century BCE, rest atop their own coffin, called a sarcophagus, *from the Greek words meaning "flesh eater."*

By comparing these paintings with those in Greek art, we can see that women went out more in Etruscan society than they did in ancient Greece. Etruscan paintings even show wives with their husbands at sporting events where male athletes competed in the nude. If you go to the Etruscan city of Tarquinia, north of Rome, you can climb down into more than a dozen Etruscan graves and see the brightly colored wall paintings still in place. They show men hunting, fishing, and wrestling. They show banquets, funerals, and religious rituals, all accompanied by music and dancing. The Etruscans loved the trumpet, the lyre, and especially the flute, which they played during hunting expeditions and athletic events, and even when they beat a disobedient slave.

Like most ancient peoples, the Etruscans believed that many gods and demons ruled the world. The gods showed their power in nature—in people, rivers, mountains, and trees. The Etruscans also adopted the characteristics of many Greek gods for their own gods. Like Zeus of the Greeks, their chief god Tinia spoke in the roar of thunder as he flung his lightning bolts across the sky. Next in power were two goddesses, Uni and Menrva. Every Etruscan city had temples to these three gods. The Romans later took over Tinia, Uni, and Menrva and called them Jupiter, Juno, and Minerva.

The Etruscans believed that their gods controlled human destiny, and priests looked to nature for omens—signs of what might happen in the future. They sought clues in lightning or the flight of certain birds. Their priests also studied the bloody livers of sacrificed sheep to learn the gods' plans for the future. They read good news or bad in the spots and discolorations they saw there.

By 600 BCE, the Etruscans were the most powerful people on the Italian peninsula. Rome's last three kings were Etruscan, and Etruscan power stretched all the way into southern Italy. But about 500 BCE, the Roman army drove out the last Etruscan king. Around the same time, a group of Greek cities banded together to defeat the Etruscan army in southern Italy. With these losses, Etruscan civilization began a slow, but sure, decline.

KEEPING THE GODS HAPPY

Many ancient peoples—Egyptians, Mesopotamians, Greeks, Hebrews, Chinese, Indians, as well as Etruscans and Romans—sacrificed animals as part of their religions. "Sacrifice" comes from two Latin words: *sacer* (holy) and *facere* (to make), so a sacrifice makes something holy, by giving it up or even killing it. A priest would kill an animal and then burn it on an altar. This was done in order to please their gods or to convince them not to be angry. When Romans sacrificed bulls, pigs, and sheep to the gods, they were trying to make a deal: *"Do ut des,"* they said, which means: "I give this to you, so that you will give something to me."

A worshiper kneels next to the Temple of Mars the Avenger to sacrifice a bull.

CHAPTER 3

LIVY

MORALITY, TYRANNY, HEROES, AND KINGS

THE BEGINNINGS OF THE REPUBLIC

All Rome knew Lucretia for her beauty and goodness. No one doubted that she loved her husband and was faithful to him. In the eyes of the average Roman, this made her a perfect woman. But to Sextus, the king's ruthless son, Lucretia's goodness was a challenge. As the Roman historian Livy tells the tale, Sextus couldn't see such perfect devotion without wanting to destroy it. Sextus went to Lucretia's house when he knew that her husband was out of town. Because Sextus was a prince and also her husband's cousin, Lucretia and her servants welcomed him and served him dinner. They didn't suspect his cruel plan.

When everyone else was asleep, Sextus crept, sword in hand, into Lucretia's bedroom. He threatened to kill her and spread a rumor that she had been unfaithful to her husband, if she refused to do what he wanted. Lucretia was not afraid of death, but she didn't want to die with her husband thinking that she hadn't been faithful to him. So she obeyed Sextus—she felt that she had no choice.

The next morning, overcome with grief and shame, Lucretia sent messengers to her husband and her father. She asked them to come right away—something terrible had happened. The men came as quickly as they could. Lucretia's husband brought along his friend Brutus. When Lucretia saw them, she began to cry and told them what Sextus had done. According to Livy, she said, "Give

Livy, *From the Founding of the City*, 25 BCE

me your right hand in faith that you will not allow the guilty to escape."

Lucretia's husband and Brutus believed in Lucretia's innocence and promised to get even with Sextus. Brutus made this solemn promise. "By this blood, which was so pure . . . I swear before you, O gods, to chase out the king . . . with his criminal wife and all their children, . . . and never to tolerate kings in Rome evermore."

Livy, *From the Founding of the City,* 25 BCE

Brutus kept his promise. He and Lucretia's husband won the loyalty of the army and drove out Sextus's father, the tyrant Tarquin the Proud—Rome's third Etruscan king. They condemned him and his whole family to life in exile, never again to see Rome. And that was the end of kingship in Rome. From this point on, kingship became so unpopular that *rex* (king) became a term of hatred and dishonor. The arrogant king Tarquin had always been unpopular. But the Romans prized high morals above all, and his son's attack on a woman's honor was the last straw.

The story of Lucretia is one explanation for how kingship ended in Rome. But how had it begun? The Romans believed that Romulus became Rome's first king when he founded the city in 753 BCE. They believed that six more kings ruled Rome until Brutus forced Tarquin the Proud from his throne in 509 BCE. According to tradition, the first

THE MORAL OF THE STORY

The Romans used stories about their founders and past heroes to display the virtues that they believed were important. People do the same thing today when they tell the story about George Washington chopping down his father's cherry tree, for example. Then and now, some of these stories were literally, exactly true; others were exaggerated—tall tales. Later Romans used the legend of Lucretia to teach right and wrong. For a woman, "right" meant faithfulness and devotion to her husband. For a man, it meant the kind of patriotism, loyalty, selflessness, and courage displayed by Brutus when he came to the aid of his friends. "Wrong" meant the arrogance of Tarquin and the brutality of Sextus.

When Lucretia died, the Roman people gathered to grieve the loss of this pure and honorable heroine.

senex = "old man" Senators were usually old men who were the heads of families.

three kings who followed Romulus to the throne were Romans. But Roman kingship was not passed down in a royal family, as it is in Great Britain, for example. Instead, when a Roman king died, the **Senate**—a group of wealthy men who owned land—elected the next ruler. Even a foreigner could rule if he could gather enough support among the senators. And that's exactly what happened when the Senate elected an Etruscan, as the fifth king of Rome. Tarquinius Priscus, later known as Tarquinius the Elder, ruled well and brought Etruscan engineering and artistry to Rome. But his grandson Lucius Tarquinius, also called Tarquin the Proud, was another story. He was the tyrant who ruled as Rome's seventh and last king.

Though no one can say for certain how many kings ruled Rome, archaeologists can prove that kings did rule Rome during this period. A 6th-century cup found in the Roman Forum at the *Regia* (the king's house) offers proof. On it is written the word *rex,* Latin for king. A black stone called the Lapis Niger gives more evidence. Also inscribed with the word *rex*, this stone probably marked the grave of an early king buried in the Forum. Ancient ruins show that the *Regia* burned down around 500 BCE. Perhaps Brutus and his followers set fire to it in their anger against Tarquin the Proud and his family.

Res + *publica* = "thing" + "of the people" A republic belongs to its people, not to a king or queen.

Once the kings were banished, the senators took control of the government. They agreed to share the leadership with the Assembly so that no one could ever again take over and rule as a tyrant. Rome became a **republic**—a state in which highest power belongs to the citizens. Its Popular Assembly was made up of the citizens who were entitled to vote: landowning men. (Slaves and women could not vote.)

Each year the Assembly elected two senators to the high office of consul. In the early years of the Republic, these men handled nearly everything. They served as judges, priests, military commanders, and city councilors. But as Rome's population grew, the workload grew too. The city needed more officials, whom they called magistrates. The consuls were still the most powerful magistrates, but the Assembly also elected other officials for the less important jobs. Praetors judged lawsuits. Aediles directed road-building projects and managed the city's markets. But no Roman official could serve for two years in a row. The Romans did not want anyone to become too popular.

Once a man had served as a magistrate, he automatically became a lifetime member of the Senate, the most powerful "club" in Rome. The Senate controlled Rome's treasury, and no money could be spent without Senate approval. The senators ordered public buildings to be built or repaired. They also investigated major crimes against the state, made foreign policy, and chose Rome's foreign ambassadors. In theory, the citizens' Assembly was the supreme authority. But since the Senate contained nearly all the experienced ex-magistrates, it usually controlled the Assembly. In reality the Senate, not the Assembly, dominated Rome's political life.

Scholars believe that this bronze bust depicts Brutus—the man who avenged Lucretia's death. After Brutus overthrew the Etruscan king, he became the first consul of Rome.

The Roman Republic lasted for five centuries. During that time Rome grew from a city of about 35,000 into a huge city, a metropolis with 1 million inhabitants and an empire with 50 million subjects. Such tremendous growth never happens without war and conquest. Rome's armies stayed busy throughout the years of the Republic. But Rome was not always the attacker. Its neighbors often besieged the city as well.

In 475 BCE, about 35 years after the Roman army had banished Tarquin the Proud, the Etruscans again threatened Rome. Livy tells the story of a soldier named Horatius Cocles who was guarding a bridge across the Tiber River when the Etruscans suddenly attacked. Horatius saw a huge band of enemy soldiers charging down the hill on the other side of the river. They were heading straight for his bridge—and Rome.

The Romans were completely outnumbered, and the men with Horatius panicked. They threw their weapons on the ground and started running. Horatius begged them to stay and fight. He said it would be foolish to run away, leaving the enemy free to cross the bridge and march into Rome. Shouting over the noise of battle, he asked them at least to destroy the bridge, if they were too afraid to fight. He would meet the enemy alone on the other side.

Horatius's courage astonished Romans and Etruscans alike, but only two Roman soldiers were brave enough to cross the bridge and fight beside him. The three men fought on the riverbank while the rest of the Romans hacked away at the bridge with their swords. When only a small strip of bridge was left, Horatius insisted that his two companions return across it to safety.

Livy, *From the Founding of the City,* 25 BCE

Livy tells the story of how Horatius stood alone, facing the enemy: "Looking round with eyes dark with menace upon the Etruscan chiefs, he challenged them to single combat, calling them the slaves of a tyrant king. . . ." At first the Etruscans held back, but then, shamed by Horatius's courage, they began to hurl their javelins at him. Horatius caught their weapons on his shield. "As stubborn as ever, he stood on the bridge, his feet planted wide apart. The Etruscans were about to charge him when two sounds split the air: the crash of the broken bridge and the cheer of the Romans when they saw the bridge fall."

This stopped the Etruscans in their tracks. Then Horatius prayed to the god of the river. "'Holy Father Tiber . . . receive these arms and your soldier into your kindly waters.' With that, he jumped into the river with all his armor on and safely swam across to his friends: an act of daring more famous than believable in later times." The Roman people placed a statue in the public square to honor

The Roman Forum encloses the remains of the sixth-century BCE public market as well as temples and other ancient buildings, both public and commercial. The Senate and Assembly met there, and the high priest and Vestal Virgins lived there.

Horatius. As a reward for his amazing courage, they gave him as much land as he could plow in a day.

Patriotic writers like Livy took great pride in telling about brave Horatius and how he stopped the foreign attackers. Livy knew that the story was exaggerated and that his first-century readers wouldn't completely believe it. But he wasn't telling it to get the facts straight. He told it because it painted a picture of Roman courage at its best. Horatius represented the "true Roman."

Even though Rome had abolished kingship, the Senate had the power to appoint a **dictator** in times of great danger. This happened in 458 BCE when the Aequi, an Italic tribe living west of Rome, attacked. The Senate sent for Cincinnatus, a farmer who had served as a consul two years earlier. The Senate's messengers found him working in his field and greeted him. They asked him to put on his toga so they might give him an important message from the Senate. Cincinnatus "asked them, in surprise, if all was well, and bade his wife, Racilia, to bring him his toga. . . . Wiping off the dust and perspiration, he put it on and came forward." Then the messengers congratulated Cincinnatus and told him that he had been appointed dictator of Rome.

"Dictate" comes from the word *dictare,* which means to recite or command. Although a Roman dictator had absolute power, his term was limited to a maximum of six months.

Livy, *From the Founding of the City,* 25 BCE

Cincinnatus immediately went to the city and set to work. Although he could have ruled as dictator for six months, Cincinnatus assembled an army, defeated the Aequi, and then laid down his power to return to his plow—all in just 15 days.

For two more centuries the Romans fought against the other peoples of Italy. Scholars follow the Romans in calling these non-Romans Italians. The Romans saw them as enemies to be conquered, even though some of them also spoke Latin.

By 266 BCE, Rome controlled the entire Italian peninsula. Roman writers used the stories of Cincinnatus and Horatius to show how courage and determination helped Rome conquer all of Italy and eventually the rest of the Mediterranean world.

“ LIVY AND EURIPIDES

CHAPTER 4

THE REBELLION OF THE POOR

CLASS CONFLICT AND THE TWELVE TABLES

plebeius = "of the common people" Today, the word plebeian describes someone who is crude or lowly. In ancient Rome, it just meant "not an aristocrat."

It was 493 BCE, and Rome's wealthy landowners were in a panic. They had held the reins of government of the new Republic while the workers (also called **plebeians**—or plebs, for short) farmed the land. The workers claimed that the rich were useless—that they did nothing except wait for the hardworking poor to feed and serve them. The landowners ignored these complaints at first.

But the plebeians began to abandon their plows and move into the city. There they became craftsmen, traders, and hired workers. As city folk, they no longer had to depend completely upon the landowners for survival. Now they were free to complain and demand greater equality between rich and poor. Justice, they believed, should be the same for everyone. And so they took action. They left the city in huge

A farm worker bends to gather grapes that have fallen in his master's orchard. The workers were poor; the landowners whom they served were rich.

numbers and went to the Sacred Mount, a hilltop several miles northeast of Rome. This got the landowners' attention!

Suddenly, the fear of war loomed large. What if an enemy attacked Rome? The landowners, also called **patricians**, could provide the generals to lead an army. But what good is a general with no men to command, no soldiers to fight? What's more: with the workers gone, who would make sandals, weave cloth, tend chickens, and sell fish? Who would run the roadside inns, bake bread, drive mules, load wagons, and dye cloth for beautiful clothes? Rome couldn't survive without the work of ordinary citizens, and the aristocrats knew it.

patria = "fatherland"
"Patrician" is related to the Latin words for father *(pater)* and fatherland *(patria)*. In ancient Rome, the patricians were wealthy landowners who claimed the founding fathers of Rome as their ancestors.

The historian Livy tells how Rome's leaders solved the crisis of the workers' walkout. They sent Agrippa Menenius, a smooth talker who was popular with the people, to the Sacred Mount to talk to the rebels. Menenius told them a story about an imaginary time when each body part had its own ideas and could talk to one another. But the body parts didn't always agree and sometimes refused to work together. For example, the hands of this strange body sometimes argued with the feet, and the mouth sometimes disagreed with the teeth.

Menenius told the rebels that one time the various parts of this body became angry at the stomach and ganged up against it. They claimed that

> it was unfair that they should have all the worry, trouble, and work of providing for the belly, while the belly had . . . nothing to do but enjoy the good things they gave it. So they plotted that the hands should carry no more food to the mouth and that the . . . teeth would refuse to chew.

" Livy, *From the Founding of the City,* 25 BCE

The body parts meant to punish the belly, but they all grew weak from lack of food. "They finally figured out that the belly had an important job after all. It received nourishment, but it also gave nourishment. It was no idle task to provide the body parts with what they all needed to survive and thrive." Using this fanciful story, Menenius convinced the workers that their rebellion would be a disaster for everyone, rich and poor alike. Rome needed all of its people.

Thanks to Menenius, the workers agreed to go home. But they refused to go back to the *status quo*. One of the plebs' chief complaints was that the law favored the patricians. And since the courts were in the hands of the rich, a poor person had no protection against an unjust judge. A judge could protect his friends or rule according to his own best interests—whatever was best for him. After the plebs made their stand at the Sacred Mount, the Senate voted to give them an assembly of their own and representatives to protect them against injustice. These officials, "tribunes of the plebs," spoke up for the people and even had the right to **veto** decrees of the Senate.

veto = "I forbid"
The Romans used the veto to keep any one person or group from becoming too powerful. The United States government uses the veto for the same reason. For instance, the President has the power to veto a bill passed by the Congress.

The plebs still complained that there were no written laws. And a poor-but-free man who owed money could still be forced into slavery if he couldn't pay his debts. So the plebs left the city again about 450 BCE. This protest finally convinced the Senate to create a written set of laws: the Twelve Tables. These laws set down, in writing, the accepted practices of the day. They didn't get to the root of the trouble between patricians and the discontented poor. The poor were still not treated as equals to the landowning rich. But the Twelve Tables were, at least, a start.

The Twelve Tables were completed in 450 BCE. At some point—no one knows exactly when—they were inscribed on 12 bronze tablets that were set up in the Forum for everyone to see. About a third of these early laws have survived because they were copied down by later writers. The others have been lost. The laws that we know about cover all sorts of crimes and conditions. Table 7, for example, decreed that if a road was not in good condition, a man

Cornelius Atimetus (right), a Roman knife maker, shows a customer his wares in front of his shop. This man, like many first century BCE craftsmen, wanted this tombstone to show his occupation.

These delicate scales found in the ruins of Pompeii probably weighed ingredients for medical prescriptions.

could legally drive his oxen across someone else's fields. Table 8 dealt with a more serious question: whether a homeowner had the right to kill a burglar who broke into his house. According to Roman law, he did—but only if the burglar came at night or if a daytime burglar was armed and tried to defend himself.

Many of the laws make sense. For example, a property owner could be forced to trim his trees so that his neighbors would get sunlight. And if someone stole money, he could not be forced to repay more than three times the amount that he stole. But others seem incredibly harsh: for example, capital punishment for a person who sang an insulting song or lied in court. But all Roman citizens had the right to appeal to the Assembly to reverse a death sentence.

Although the silver-tongued Agrippa Menenius had settled the first revolt of the plebs, the struggle between patricians and plebeians lasted for centuries. The plebs kept fighting for greater justice. Though the law still favored the rich, the new written laws were much fairer than the old ones that were based on custom. As the Greek poet Euripides wrote in the fifth century BCE, "When laws are written, rich and poor get equal justice."

A code of laws similar to the Twelve Tables was written in Athens sometime earlier. Like the Twelve Tables, this code was an attempt to ease the tensions between the upper and lower classes.

“ Euripides, *The Suppliants*, 422 BCE

CHAPTER 5

FATHERS, GODS, AND GODDESSES

RELIGION IN ANCIENT ROME

TOMB, SARCOPHAGUS, AND STATUE FROM ROME; AULUS GELLIUS; AND LIVY

Cornelius Scipio Hispanus was not a modest man. He praised not only himself, but his whole family as well. When he died around 135 BCE, the epitaph written on his tomb listed his many elected offices, followed by four lines of poetry, bragging about his accomplishments:

Tomb from Rome, 135 BCE

> By my good conduct, I heaped
> honor upon the honor of my family;
> I had children, and I tried to equal
> the deeds of my father;
> I won the praise of my ancestors
> and made them glad I was born;
> My own virtue has made noble my
> family tree.

For generations, the Scipio men had served in high offices. And by the second century BCE, the Scipios had become Rome's leading family. They decorated their family tomb with marble busts of important family members. The oldest sarcophagus contains the body of a Scipio who was a consul of Rome in 298 BCE. Its dedication reads: "Lucius Cornelius Scipio Barbatus, son of Gnaeus, a brave and wise man, whose handsomeness matched his bravery. He was consul, censor, and aedile among you. He captured . . . many cities for Rome and brought home hostages."

Statue from Rome, 50–25 BCE

Sarcophagus from Rome, 298 BCE

Like other patricians, Scipio Hispanus proudly claimed his ancestors as founding fathers of Rome. He was probably much like the Roman in this statue. Even though scholars cannot tell us this person's name, we can learn a lot just by looking at him. First: he's a Roman. We know because he's wearing a toga, the garment that was a sign of manhood. The Romans called it the ***toga virilis,*** and a boy wasn't allowed to wear it until he became a man, usually at 16. Second, because this unknown Roman is carrying masks of his ancestors, we know that his father or grandfather had served as one of Rome's top officials.

vir = "man"
Roman boys donned the *toga virilis* when they became men. *Virilis* is a form of *vir;* "virile" means "manly."

These masks, made of wax or clay, usually hung in the hallways of the ancestral home. Romans took them down and carried them in parades and funeral processions.

Roman families were organized like miniature states, with their own religion and governments. The oldest man in the family was called the **paterfamilias**, the patriarch. He was the boss, and his words were law. Scipio Hispanus was the paterfamilias in his family. This meant that he held lifelong power, even over life and death. He could sell or kill a disobedient slave. He had the right to abandon an unwanted baby, leaving him or her outside to die. Usually this would be a sick child or a baby girl to whom the family couldn't afford to give a dowry when she grew up. Romans wanted healthy sons to carry on the family name, yet a father could imprison, whip, disown, or even execute a son who committed a crime. In 63 BCE, a senator named Aulus Fulvius did exactly that after his son took part in a plot to overthrow the government. But this didn't happen very often. Roman fathers were expected to rule their families with justice and mercy, the same way that political leaders were expected to rule the state.

pater + *familias* = "father" + "family"
The paterfamilias was the oldest male member of a Roman family.

For both the family and the state, religion played a major role in life. Every Roman home had a shrine to the household gods, the Lares. The father served as the family's priest. Scipio Hispanus would have led his family's prayers and made sacrifices to honor their ancestors and please the gods that protected the entire family—living and dead. When a baby was born, Scipio Hispanus would have hit the threshold of his home with an axe and a broom to frighten away any wild spirits that might try to sneak in. When a household member died, family members carried the body out feet first to make sure that its ghost didn't run back inside. (That's why people still sometimes describe death as "going out feet first.")

TOMBS OF THE SCIPIOS

The Romans believed that the dead should neither be buried nor cremated inside the city walls. They were afraid that Rome's sacred places would become polluted by the presence of death. So they lined the roads leading away from Rome with monuments built to house and honor the dead. Visitors can still see the tombs of the Scipios buried along the Appian Way, about two miles from the Forum. (The Appian Way is a military road that was built in the fourth century BCE.)

One of the most important household gods was Janus, the Spirit of the Door. Janus had two faces. One looked into the home; the other faced the outside world. He let friends and family in but kept enemies out. Family life began and ended with him. Vesta ruled as the goddess of the fireplace. She was the spirit inside the flame that cooked food and kept the family warm. When Scipio Hispanus married, and later when babies were born, he would have presented the new family members to Vesta so that she would know to protect them as well.

Each day, the whole family gathered at the hearth and tossed salt and flour onto the flames. These gifts of salt and flour symbolized the basic needs of life. Scipio Hispanus, like all Roman fathers, had to keep the household gods happy. Rulers and leaders had the same job for the community. They tried to keep peace with the gods through public celebrations that included prayers, festivals, and sacrifices.

In the earliest times, it was the king's job to keep the gods happy and make sure they stayed on Rome's side. Later, consuls performed these traditional rituals and ceremonies. As Rome grew and its society became more complicated, priests and priestesses took over the religious responsibilities. They served in the temples of the gods. In the temple to Vesta, for example, the Vestal Virgins tended the city's hearth and guarded the holy flame where Vesta lived. Her priestesses made vows of chastity, promising not to have sexual relationships during the 30 years they served the goddess.

Aulus Gellius, a Roman lawyer of the second century CE, writes about Vesta's priestesses.

“ Aulus Gellius, *Attic Nights*, 180 CE

> A girl chosen to be a Vestal Virgin must . . . be no younger than six and no older than ten years old. . . . As soon as a girl is chosen, she is taken to the House of Vesta and handed over to the priests. She immediately leaves her father's control.

The chief duty of the Vestal Virgins was to keep Vesta's flame burning. If the flame went out, it meant that one of the

Vestal Virgins had been careless in her sacred duties or had broken her vow of chastity. Either way, the Romans believed that the city was in great danger and could be destroyed. They dressed the offending priestess in funeral clothes and carried her to an underground cell, leaving her to die.

The earliest Romans were farmers who saw the gods in all the forces of nature. They believed that gods ruled the

BORROWED GODS

ROMAN GOD	GREEK NAME	ROLE
Jupiter	Zeus	*King of the gods, the spirit of the sky*
Juno	Hera	*Queen of the gods*
Venus	Aphrodite	*Goddess of love and beauty*
Mars	Ares	*God of war*
Minerva	Athena	*Goddess of wisdom*
Mercury	Hermes	*Messenger god and god of merchants*
Pluto	Hades	*God of the underworld*
Diana	Artemis	*Goddess of the forest and of the hunt*
Ceres	Demeter	*Goddess of grain*
Saturn	Cronos	*God of agriculture*
Bacchus	Dionysus	*God of wine*

MISNUMBERED MONTHS

In the Roman calendar, some months were named for gods and goddesses: Janus, Mars, Maia, and Juno—our January, March, May, and June. Other months were numbered: Quintilius, Sextilius, September, October, November, and December. (Roman numbers go like this: *unus* = 1; *duo* = 2; *tres* = 3; *quattuor* = 4; *quintus* = 5; *sextus* = 6; *septem* = 7; *octo* = 8; *novem* = 9; *decem* = 10) Quintilius and Sextilius started as numbered months, but they were later renamed for the Roman leaders Julius Caesar and Augustus—our July and August.

But why does September come from the Latin word for 7, when it's the 9th month in our calendar? And why do October, November, and December—our 10th, 11th, and 12th months—come from the Latin words for 8, 9, and 10? Because in very ancient times—before Julius Caesar revised the calendar—the Roman year began in March.

sun, the moon, and the planets and that gods lived within the trees, in wind, and in rivers. These early, simple beliefs played a part in Rome's later religion as well. But as Rome became more connected with other peoples through war and trade, its religion became more complex.

The Romans were as quick to borrow religion from other peoples as they were to borrow language and inventions. If they encountered a new god that they thought might be useful, they adopted him or her. For example, when the Romans attacked the Etruscan city of Veii in 396 BCE, they begged Juno, their enemy's goddess, to help them in battle. "To you, Juno Regina, who now lives in Veii, I pray that after our victory you will accompany us to our city—soon to be your city—to be received in a temple worthy of your greatness." When the Romans conquered Veii, they assumed that Juno had helped them. To thank the goddess, they built a temple in her honor in Rome.

“ Livy, *From the Founding of the City,* 25 BCE

Rome borrowed the Olympian gods from Greece, where they were thought to live on Mount Olympus. Eventually, the Romans had gods for almost everything. They prayed to Juno for help with the birth of a baby, to Mars for help in battle, to Jupiter before planting their crops, and to Ceres for a good yield of grain.

Roman religion, government, and family were all closely connected. Each reflected the other. Jupiter ruled over the gods as father and king—just as kings and consuls ruled the Roman state and fathers ruled their families.

With her head veiled, the Spirit of the Family stands between the two Lares to offer a sacrifice. Household shrines such as this one were the focus of the family's religious celebrations.

CHAPTER 6

HANNIBAL, ROME'S WORST ENEMY

THE BATTLE FOR THE MEDITERRANEAN

LIVY AND POLYBIUS

"Hannibal, then about nine years old, was . . . pestering Hamilcar to take him along to Spain. His father, who was sacrificing to the gods before crossing over into Spain with his army, led the boy up to the altar and made him touch the offerings."

Livy, *From the Founding of the City*, 25 BCE

What would these offerings have been? Hamilcar Barca, a powerful North African general, would probably have sacrificed a black dog whose body he had split in two with his sword, along with a white bull and a ewe whose throats he had slit. After killing the animals, he would have burned them on an altar so the gods could enjoy the smell of meat roasting in the flames. Military leaders made such sacrifices to persuade the gods to give them victory over their enemies. Livy tells us that as Hannibal touched the bodies of the slaughtered animals, Hamilcar made him "solemnly swear . . . that as soon as he was able, he would become the declared enemy of the Roman people."

Livy, *From the Founding of the City*, 25 BCE

Hannibal kept the promise that he had made to his father. He became a great general. And in 217 BCE, he took war elephants from Carthage (in modern

This 18th-century statue shows a proud and powerful Hannibal, dressed and armed as the hero of the Carthaginians.

Tunisia), his hometown in North Africa, and marched to the gates of Rome. Rome had never faced a more dangerous enemy in all of its long history.

Who were these Carthaginians who hated the Romans so much? They were seafaring people who left their homeland in Phoenicia (modern-day Lebanon) around 800 BCE. They set up colonies in North Africa and Spain, and also on the island of Sicily—the ball that the Italian boot seems to be kicking.

media + *terra* = "middle" + "land" The Romans first called it *mare nostrum,* "our sea." Later, they called it the Mediterranean—"in the middle of the land"—because, by then, the Empire completely encircled the sea.

The most powerful Phoenician colony was the North African city of Carthage. It became a busy trading post for merchants from all over the **Mediterranean** world. In time, Carthage gained independence from its mother country, conquered other Phoenician colonies, and founded colonies of its own. By the 3rd century BCE, this thriving and wealthy city controlled trade across the western Mediterranean.

Like two bullies on the same playground, Rome and Carthage both wanted to be *the* power in the western

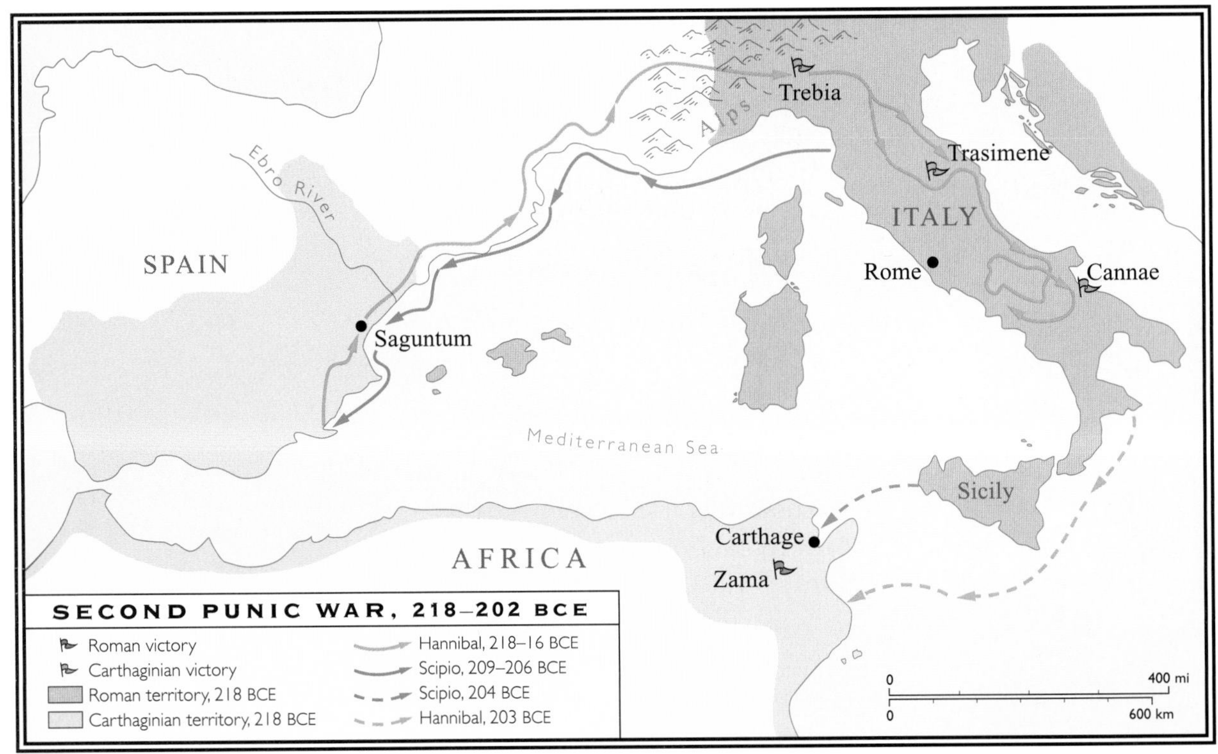

Mediterranean world. They both wanted to dominate the fertile island of Sicily and control trade at the Straits of Messina, between Sicily and the Italian mainland. Even before Hannibal's time, the clash between the two cities was brewing. Although both cities were strong and proud, they were very different. Rome's army had already conquered all of Italy. Yet Carthage was wealthier and had a much better navy.

A titanic struggle between Rome and Carthage began in 264 BCE—17 years before Hannibal was born. It started when the Sicilian city of Messina asked Rome to join in its fight against Syracuse, another city in Sicily. Then Syracuse asked Carthage to join in its fight against Messina and Rome. A series of wars raged, on and off, for a century, with these two military alliances fighting against one another. These were called the Punic Wars, from the Latin word for Phoenica. The enemies fought one another in Italy, Spain, Sicily, and North Africa.

At the beginning of the First Punic War, the Romans had no navy, only trading ships. They didn't even know how to fight on the sea. They only knew how to fight on land, so they invented a grappling machine that made sea battles more like land battles. The machine had huge hooks with heavy ropes attached. The Roman soldier-sailors lobbed the hooks over the side of an enemy ship. The hooks bit into the other ship, holding it while the Romans pulled it up beside their own. With the enemy's ship locked in place, the Romans scrambled aboard and fought hand-to-hand on deck. This technique literally gave the Romans a "fighting chance" at sea.

In 241 BCE, a Roman commander attacked a Carthaginian fleet of 170 ships. Despite stormy seas, Rome sank 50 enemy ships and captured 70 more. What was left of the Carthaginian fleet sailed home, defeated. When the ships arrived in their home port, the commander was executed.

After 23 years of battle, the First Punic War was over. Rome controlled Sicily and dominated the western Mediterranean. The Roman army had broken Carthage's grip. The memory of this shameful defeat tortured Hannibal's father.

THE PUNIC WARS

8th century BCE
Rome and Carthage are both founded

264–241 BCE
Rome fights Carthage in First Punic War

220 BCE
Hannibal lays siege to Saguntum

218 BCE
Rome declares war on Carthage again

216 BCE
Hannibal defeats the Romans at Cannae

202 BCE
Scipio Africanus defeats Hannibal at Zama

146 BCE
Scipio's grandson completes destruction of Carthage

MIGHTY WAR ELEPHANTS

A full-grown horse weighs, on average, about 1,000 pounds. Male elephants weigh between 9,000 and 14,000 pounds, depending upon the breed. They measure about 12 feet tall, from their shoulders to the ground.

Hannibal's huge, painted elephants astonished everyone who saw them on the long march to Italy. Imagine the terror of the soldiers who faced them in battle.

As part of the peace treaty, Rome demanded that Carthage pay 80 tons of silver—equal to a year's pay for 200,000 Roman soldiers. The city had to find some way to pay this huge bill. Carthage sent its top general, Hamilcar Barca, to Spain. His assignment was to conquer the region and develop the silver and copper mines there. Hamilcar took his son Hannibal to Spain with him, and he did his job well. He sent money and goods back to Carthage.

When Hamilcar died, the 26-year-old Hannibal took over the job. Like his father, Hannibal considered Spain to be *his* territory. He believed Carthage must be the only power there. So when Rome made an alliance with the Spanish city of Saguntum, Hannibal fought back and fulfilled the promise he had made as a boy: to be the sworn enemy of Rome. He laid siege to Saguntum, cutting off all supplies of food and military aid. After eight months, Saguntum fell to Hannibal's warriors. And in 218 BCE, Rome declared war on Carthage—again. The Second Punic War had begun.

The Romans planned to invade Spain and fight Hannibal there. But Hannibal didn't wait around. He decided to surprise them and invade Italy first. The journey toward Rome took five months, beginning with a long march across France. Then Hannibal led his soldiers through the Alps. He lost one-third of his men during the icy mountain crossing. But still he marched on, with men, horses, and war elephants. These African elephants were decorated for battle and painted in bright colors. (Their trunks were usually red.) Swords were attached to their tusks. Some carried towers on their backs—small fortresses that protected the soldiers riding inside as they shot arrows and hurled stones at their Roman enemies.

The Romans first faced Hannibal's elephants at the Battle of Lake Trebia in northern Italy in 218 BCE. When Hannibal gave the signal, the elephant handlers jabbed the beasts with iron pokers—whips are not enough for elephants—and drove the trumpeting animals forward. Most Italians had never seen an elephant. Their size alone must have been terrifying. The Roman horses—and many soldiers too—panicked at the sight and smell of these monstrous creatures.

Pressing deeper into Italy, Hannibal showed his cleverness at the Battle of Lake Trasimene, in central Italy, in 217 BCE. Pretending to march against Rome itself, he lured the Romans into a narrow pass and ambushed them from the hills. His troops demolished the Roman army.

A year later, Hannibal conquered the Roman troops again at the Battle of Cannae, in southern Italy, thanks to his powerful **cavalry** and a brilliant battle plan. Hannibal commanded the soldiers fighting in the center to pretend to retreat—to move back, as if they were losing. The Romans fell for Hannibal's trick and followed. Then the Carthaginians fighting on the flanks closed in on the Romans and surrounded them. The Romans were trapped!

caballus = "horse" Cavalry are soldiers on horseback.

Rome lost nearly 60,000 soldiers. Another 10,000 were captured. Fewer than 6,000 Carthaginians fell in the battle. The Romans had never suffered a worse defeat and they were terrified. Whenever a watchman thought he spotted an army approaching the city, his cry, *"Hannibal ad portas"* ("Hannibal at the gates") would echo through the streets. But the stunning defeat at Cannae became a turning point. More and more men joined the Roman military, and wealthy citizens gave generously to the war effort. The leaders in the Senate decided not to meet Hannibal in fixed battles, but to let him wear himself out in smaller battles in the countryside.

Rome's new battle plan worked. The Carthaginian troops became exhausted. Hannibal's soldiers had been in Italy for more than 10 years, and Carthage refused to send fresh troops. When the Roman general Publius Cornelius Scipio took charge of the Roman forces in Spain, he cut

Scipio Africanus, sculpted in black marble, has a firmly set jaw, which shows the determination that brought him victory over Hannibal.

THE LOST CITY

Despite its one-time glory, historians cannot give us a very full picture of Carthage and its people. This is because the city was completely destroyed in 146 BCE. And there are almost no Carthaginian writings left. Our only sources, other than archaeological finds, are the writings of Carthage's Greek and Roman enemies.

Enemies don't paint flattering pictures. The Greek historian Diodorus Siculus, writing in the 1st century CE, was shocked by some of the things the Carthaginians did. He wrote that they had slaughtered 500 children on the altar of their chief god, Baal. And in 1976 archaeologists found proof: hundreds of vases with the bones of young children inside.

As Carthage Burned

The Greek historian Polybius was with the younger Scipio when Carthage finally burned to the ground. In his eyewitness account, Polybius wrote that his friend Scipio wept to see such a great and beautiful city demolished.

Scipio . . . reflected on the inevitable change which awaits every city, nation, and kingdom, as it does every one of us men. . . . When I asked him boldly what he meant, he grasped my hand and said, "O Polybius, I am terrified that one day someone will give an order to destroy my own city."

off Hannibal's supplies of food and equipment. The Romans finally drove the Carthaginians out of Spain in 206 BCE. Then they invaded North Africa and the town of Zama, to the southwest of Carthage. Hannibal faced Scipio in the fierce Battle of Zama in 202 BCE.

At Zama, Scipio ordered his soldiers to attack Hannibal's frontline elephants with spears and arrows. The elephants panicked and turned back, crashing into the soldiers behind them. Scipio's army killed almost all of the Carthaginians, but Hannibal survived. Under Roman pressure he fled Carthage and spent his last 15 years in exile. In the peace settlement between the two cities, Carthage surrendered all its possessions outside Africa. Rome gave Scipio the honorary title "Africanus," which means "conqueror of Africa."

Carthage never again threatened Rome, but many Romans continued to fear it. In 146 BCE, a half-century after the victory of Scipio Africanus, his grandson's troops finished the destruction of Carthage, Rome's last opponent in the western Mediterranean. Rome had become the dominant power on land and sea. It remained so for more than five hundred years.

Wounded soldiers fall in the midst of fierce combat, and frightened elephants trumpet and retreat in this 16th-century painting of the battle at Zama, in 202 BCE.

CHAPTER 7

A ROMAN THROUGH AND THROUGH

CATO AND GREEK CULTURE

PLUTARCH AND CICERO

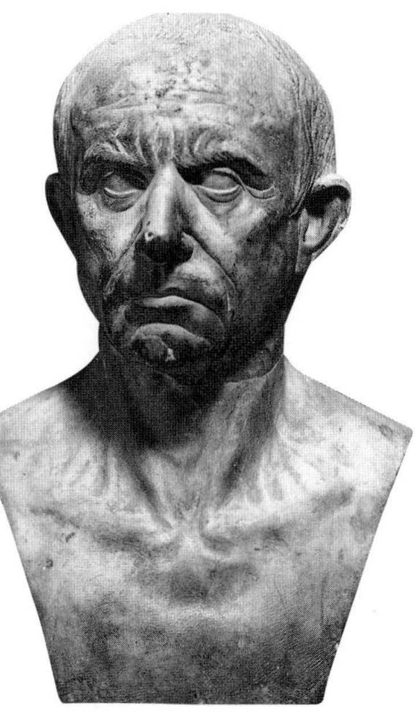

This bust of Cato the Elder shows a stern, thin man with a sad expression—perhaps because he was so often disappointed in his countrymen.

Marcus Porcius Cato was one of Rome's most recognizable figures. Red-haired, with piercing gray eyes, Cato was always ready for a fight—against his political foes in the Senate or his enemies on the battlefield. He began his life as a warrior by fighting against Hannibal when he was 17 years old. It was the first of many battles in Italy, Spain, and Greece.

Cato became one of Rome's most respected generals. When meeting an enemy, he would glare and bellow a ferocious war cry. He believed that he could begin to defeat his enemies by scaring them first.

A fighter to the end, Cato never forgot how close Carthage had come to toppling Rome. For the rest of his life he was terrified that the threat of Carthage would return. Cato made many public speeches, and he ended every one of them, no matter what it was about, with these passionate words, "And I say to you that Carthage must be destroyed." One day he brought some North African figs to the Senate. When some senators admired their freshness, he pointed out that Carthage (in modern Tunisia) was just a three-day sail from Rome—too close for Cato's comfort. Just before Cato's death in 149 BCE, Rome launched its last war against Carthage. The Romans finally destroyed the enemy city three years later.

Plutarch, *Life of Cato,* 110 CE

A Roman through and through, Cato was a devoted family man. Plutarch, a Greek biographer writing 250 years after Cato's death, reported that Cato was particularly concerned about the education of his son. "Cato himself took charge and taught him to read and write, even though he owned an accomplished slave . . . who instructed many boys. But Cato did not think it was proper for a slave to criticize his son or

Plutarch, *Life of Cato,* 110 CE

to pinch his ears when he was a slow learner." So Cato took matters into his own hands. "He was his son's reading teacher, law professor, and athletic coach. He taught his son not only how to hurl a javelin, to fight in armor, and to ride a horse, but also to box, to endure both heat and cold, and to swim strongly through the . . . river."

Cato modeled his life on the traditional values of early Rome. He believed in living simply. He wore plain clothes and drank the same wine that he gave to his slaves. He worked with his hands, farming his own land. He didn't believe in planting flower gardens, just vegetables. Nothing, he thought, should be purely for show.

Cato always ate simple foods. On active military duty, he drank no wine, only water. (Occasionally, if he was especially thirsty, he would sip a bit of vinegar.) It bothered him to see people spending money on expensive foods. Once he turned down an invitation to a fancy dinner party, saying that he didn't want to waste his time with someone who thought that a person's taste buds were more important than his heart.

“ Plutarch, *Life of Cato,* 110 CE

Plutarch says that Cato was "content with a cold breakfast, a frugal dinner, the simplest clothing, and a humble cottage to live in while working on his own land." But not all Romans shared Cato's love of the simple, old-fashioned life. Romans in Cato's time were fascinated by the richness of Greek culture. In past years Rome had learned a lot—in art, literature, and religion—from the Greek colonists who lived in southern Italy and Sicily. But at the beginning of the 2nd century BCE, the Romans came into contact with the cities and kingdoms of Greece itself. They also encountered the kingdoms of the Near East, where Greek cul-

Perched on a bluff above the Bay of Naples, this luxurious villa is an example of the extravagance that Cato hated and feared. This painting is a fresco, painted while the plaster was still wet.

The painted walls and decorative mosaic floor make this small bedroom look larger. This museum copy of a first-century BCE room includes the kind of wooden couch that Cato would have slept upon.

ture reigned. In fact, the whole eastern Mediterranean had come under Greek influence, thanks to a bold conqueror known as Alexander the Great.

Alexander came from a family of kings who ruled in Macedon, a small kingdom on Greece's northern border. Beginning in 336 BCE, when he was 20 years old, he conquered Greece, Asia Minor (now Turkey), Egypt, Bactria (Afghanistan), Mesopotamia (Iraq), and Persia (Iran). Alexander established more than 70 new Greek cities in a huge empire that stretched as far east as India. But after his death, his empire fell apart. Some of his generals carved parts of it into three separate kingdoms in Macedon, Asia, and Egypt. The generals' descendants ruled these kingdoms for centuries. Then, in the 2nd century BCE, a group of Greek cities joined forces against Macedon's king, Philip V, and asked Rome to help overthrow him.

The Greeks' request for military aid came not long after Rome had defeated its great enemy, the Carthaginian leader Hannibal. And since Philip had once been Hannibal's ally,

Rome was glad to send its armies against Philip. In 196 BCE, Rome defeated the Macedonians and declared that all Greek cities were now free and under its protecting wing.

Rome's new connection with the Greek world brought it into conflict with Antiochus III, a powerful king in Asia. While Antiochus was fighting in far-away India, some Greek cities under his control rebelled. The king wanted to regain his power over them. He might have succeeded—and the history of the Mediterranean world might have been different—if Antiochus had not welcomed a certain exiled general into his court. That general was Hannibal.

By protecting Rome's most hated enemy, Antiochus invited Rome's fury—and got it. Rome was always ready to fight against Hannibal's friends. And no Roman was readier than Cato. When Antiochus invaded Greece in 190 BCE, Cato rallied Rome against him. Led by the brother of Scipio Africanus, the hero of the Punic Wars, a Roman army drove Antiochus from Greece. Then it chased him into Asia and defeated him there.

The peace treaty that ended the war forced Antiochus to pay a huge fine. He had to give up his Indian war elephants and most of his ships. He had to pull out his troops from Asia Minor and stop protecting Hannibal. Abandoned by his last ally, Hannibal—once the terror of Rome—took his own life.

After the victory over Antiochus, Roman commanders became arrogant and ruthless in their dealings with the Greek world. Roman armies now marched against any Greek cities that opposed or offended Rome in any way. And there was no mercy for the conquered people. After it crushed a Greek rebellion in 168 BCE, for example, Rome took 1,000 young noblemen, including the historian Polybius, as hostages and kept them in Rome for 17 years. The Roman commander Aemilius Paullus later swept across northern Greece and carried off 150,000 men, women, and children as slaves.

Corinth was the last Greek city to rebel against Roman power. In 146 BCE, Rome crushed the Corinthian rebels and completely destroyed the ancient city. The victors took Corinth's treasures to Rome and sold its people into slavery.

FEED A FEVER A FROG

Romans had many recipes for homemade tonics and dishes that they believed would cure illness. Many recipes contained frogs, a popular ingredient. A thick soup made of shrimp, flour, and frog meat was recommended for people who were tired all the time. To cure a fever, Romans cooked the flesh of frogs in olive oil. And for anyone who had been bitten by a toad, crushed frogs soaked in wine made an excellent antidote to the poison.

Even though the Romans treated the Greeks with great cruelty, Rome's military commanders admired what they saw in Greece. Roman leaders wanted to live in Greek-styled elegance. They copied the Greeks when they decorated their homes, temples, and city buildings. For a Roman to speak Greek and quote from Greek literature showed that he was refined and well educated. Educated Greek captives became tutors in noble Roman families. Roman politicians also copied the Greeks in giving grand speeches, called **orations**. Even Scipio Africanus, Rome's great defender against Hannibal, imitated Greek customs and wore Greek-style clothes.

"Oration" comes from the word *orare*, which means to plead or pray. In law courts and in political speeches, Greek and Roman orators tried to persuade people to act or think in a certain way.

All of this infuriated that traditional Roman, Marcus Porcius Cato. He wanted Romans to honor and follow their city's old ways. He didn't trust the Greeks. He said "Greeks speak from the lips; Romans speak from the heart." Cato tried to keep Greek philosophers from teaching in Rome, and he didn't like to see Greek doctors practicing there. Cato warned people that Greek doctors would poison them. He advised them to stick to home remedies. He even put together a book of recipes and used them whenever anyone in his own household was ill. He gave his patients herbal mixtures and allowed them to eat nothing but small portions of duck, pigeon, and rabbit meat. Cato believed that this treatment would cure any illness, though he admitted that it often caused nightmares. (He lived to be 86 years old, so it worked for him.)

“ Plutarch, *Life of Cato*, 110 CE

Many wealthy patricians loved Greek culture and hated Cato. But to ordinary Romans, Cato was a hero. Late in life, he was elected to the office of censor.

Surgeons in ancient Rome used instruments like this iron "brush" on patients anesthetized only with wine. Common operations included pulling impacted teeth, helping women in difficult births, and removing tumors.

A censor's duties were described by the great orator Cicero, who lived about a hundred years after Cato. Cicero writes that

Cicero, *About Constitutions*, 51 BCE

> censors will record the ages, children, slaves, and property value of all citizens. They will undertake the building of temples, roads, and aqueducts in the city. . . . They will watch over the morals of the people and will allow no one who is guilty of shameless behavior to stay in the Senate.

Cato took that last part of his job very seriously: the business of watching over the morals of other people. He attacked the corruption of wealthy Romans and enforced a heavy tax on expensive clothes, carriages, furniture, and jewelry. He took legal action against wealthy people who overcharged the state on contracts or who piped water from the **aqueducts** into their own homes without paying. For this, he was known as Cato the Censor, long after his term was over.

aqua + *duco* = "water" + "to lead or direct" Hundreds of miles of aqueducts brought fresh water from nearby rivers and mountains to Rome.

Cato lived in a time of change, and he didn't like it. He saw Rome becoming more and more powerful in the Mediterranean world. He feared that wealth and the flood of slaves—and the leisure that they provided—would make the Romans grow careless, soft, and lazy. Cato devoted his life to fighting change in his beloved city.

Most of what we know about Cato comes from Plutarch, a Greek who had little respect for Cato because of Cato's hatred of foreigners. Plutarch scornfully reports that Cato "made a statement that was absurdly rash for an old man: he pronounced with all the solemnity of a prophet that if ever the Romans became infected with the literature of Greece, they would lose their empire."

Plutarch, *Life of Cato*, 110 CE

Plutarch wrote two and a half centuries after Cato's death. He had the advantage of hindsight—he had seen that Cato was wrong. Greek gods, alphabet, language, art, and architecture had already made their mark on Roman civilization, a mark that would never be erased. Rome had accepted Greek culture more since Cato's time, not less. And its civilization had not collapsed. Instead it had grown increasingly powerful.

CHAPTER 8

SPARTACUS THE REBEL

SLAVERY IN ANCIENT ROME

SLAVE COLLAR FROM ROME, DIODORUS, CATO, AND PLUTARCH

Spartacus was born into a world of comfort and freedom. His father may even have been a nobleman. And yet Spartacus died a Roman slave.

Ancient writers give us only a sketchy outline of Spartacus's early years, but he was probably born in Thrace on the eastern fringe of Rome's huge empire. He served in the Roman army for a while but then deserted. Now instead of fighting to defend Rome, he became a rebel and a robber.

When the Romans captured him, they made him a slave and put him on the auction block. Whoever offered the most money would own him. Like all slaves in ancient

The actor Kirk Douglas fights the Romans in the title role of the 1960 movie Spartacus.

Rome, Spartacus could be bought and sold as easily as a pottery bowl or a bundle of grain. If he got into trouble or tried to escape, he might be forced to wear a metal band around his neck. On one of these collars, now in a museum, are the words: "I have run away. Capture me. When you have returned me to my master . . . you will get a reward." He might have had a brand on his face, made with a sizzling-hot iron. He could not own land or vote. He could not marry legally, and his children would be born into slavery. He could not choose his work; his master would make that decision.

“ Slave collar from Rome, 4th century CE

Many foreign slaves, mostly prisoners of war, did the backbreaking work of building roads and aqueducts. Another unpleasant job was cleaning the public toilets and baths. But one of the worst places to work was in the silver mines of Spain. This was often the fate of slaves who had been convicted of crimes. The Greek historian Diodorus describes the lives of these men:

“ Diodorus, *The History of the World*, 30 BCE

> Their bodies are worn down from working in the mine shafts both day and night. Many die because of the terrible treatment they suffer. They are given no rest or break from their work but are forced by the whiplashes of their overseers to endure the most dreadful hardships. . . . They often pray more for death than for life.

In the early years of the Roman Republic, most slaves were native Italians. These were people who fell into slavery because they had money troubles and couldn't pay their debts. Later, as Rome gradually conquered the Mediterranean world, the number of slaves grew, especially during and

This coffin shows a Roman family at dinner while slaves cook and wash the pots in the kitchen below. Kitchens were in the slave quarters to keep the noise and mess away from the family's living rooms.

right after the wars between Rome and Carthage. By the first century BCE, when Spartacus lived, Rome had millions of foreign slaves.

Most of the slaves who were brought into Italy served their masters as farm laborers. Their owners thought of them as things, not human beings. Cato, writing in the second century BCE, advised his son that a "master should sell any old oxen, cattle or sheep that are not good enough, . . . an old cart or old tools, an old slave or a sick slave." For Cato, a slave was no different from a farm animal or a plow—something to be used, then thrown out when it became old or broken down.

“ Cato, *On Agriculture*, 160 BCE

Many slaves rebelled against this brutal treatment. The first huge, terrifying rebellion began in Sicily in 135 BCE when 200,000 slaves took up arms against their owners. And Spartacus led the last slave revolt in 73 BCE.

Plutarch describes Spartacus as having "great courage and great physical strength. He was very intelligent . . . more than one would expect of a slave." Because he was so strong, Spartacus was bought by a school that trained gladiators in Capua, south of Rome. The gladiators faced

“ Plutarch, *Life of Crassus*, 110 CE

SLAVES IN NORTH AMERICA

The first slaves in North America were brought to Virginia in 1619 to work in the fields and homes of wealthy farmers. Although many were trusted by their masters, they weren't often given the chance to work as teachers, craftsmen, or artists as Roman slaves so frequently were.

Slavery was abolished in the British Empire in 1833, but was not abolished in the United States until the end of the Civil War in 1865. And there are still slaves in some parts of the world today.

possible injury—sometimes death—every time they entered the arena to fight. But to the Roman audiences, these battles were "games." And if a gladiator was injured, his suffering was just part of the entertainment.

But Spartacus didn't intend to live—or die—as a slave. He secretly organized 200 gladiators in the school and together they planned a daring escape. At the last moment, the managers of the school discovered the plot and captured more than half of the men. But, according to Plutarch, Spartacus and about 70 men escaped with knives and skewers that they stole from the school's kitchen.

As the rebels slipped through the darkened streets of Capua, they got a lucky break: they happened upon a cart full of weapons, intended for use in the gladiatorial games. The men helped themselves and left the city, armed with swords and daggers. Their first hiding place was in the top of Mt. Vesuvius, an inactive volcano.

When the news broke about the slaves' escape, Rome sent 3,000 foot soldiers to surround the slaves and starve them out. Spartacus and his men were outnumbered, but not outwitted. While the Romans guarded the road, the rebels cut some thick vines they found growing near the mouth of the volcano. They twisted the vines into ropes, which they used to climb down the mountain. Surprising their enemies, they seized the Roman camp, and the defeated Romans fled.

As word of this astonishing victory spread, thousands of farm slaves left their masters and joined Spartacus. The rebel band grew to nearly 70,000 men who roamed the countryside and broke into slaves' barracks. The rebels freed thousands of men and armed them for battle against Rome and their former masters.

The Senate thought it would be easy to defeat Spartacus, but Spartacus's men defeated the Roman forces again and again. Then the senators appointed Crassus, one of Rome's top generals, as commander in chief. Crassus sent a lieutenant named Mummius against the ex-slaves. The rebels crushed Mummius so completely that he lost his soldiers, his tents, and equipment—even his horse. The soldiers who survived the battle saved their own lives by handing over their weapons to the enemy.

Crassus was furious. He armed the men again. Then he divided 500 of the soldiers into 50 groups of 10. In each group, the men drew straws, and one man was chosen. Plutarch says that Crassus ordered the death of these fifty men, that they be executed "with a variety of appalling and terrible methods, performed before the eyes of the whole army, gathered to watch." Crassus finally led Rome to victory, but only after a long, fierce struggle. Most of the rebels were killed. According to Plutarch, Spartacus refused to give up and fought savagely, even after the last of his men had deserted him. In the end, he died a soldier's death—with his sword in his hand.

Plutarch, *Life of Crassus*, 110 CE

The Romans **crucified** 6,000 rebels and left them hanging on wooden crosses all along the Appian Way—a road that led to Rome. Their rotting bodies served as a horrible warning to rebellious slaves.

crux + *figere* =
"cross" + "to fix or attach"
Crucifixion was a cruel, but common, method of execution reserved for slaves or non-citizens. The victim's hands and feet were nailed to a cross of wood, and they were left to hang until they died.

Although Rome was cruel to its slaves, not all of them suffered as terribly as the gladiators and mine workers did. Many captured people were skilled craftsmen who were allowed to continue their work as potters, artists, or metal workers. Those who worked in the homes of wealthy aristocrats were also treated fairly well—compared to less fortunate slaves. Household slaves were usually well fed and clothed. And their jobs were much safer and more pleasant. They worked as nannies, cooks, and seamstresses. Well-educated Greek slaves could become household secretaries or tutors for their masters' children.

Lucius Caltilius and his wife, Caltilia, look out proudly from their funeral altar. They were freed slaves who "hit the jackpot" in business, as shown by Caltilia's very fancy hairdo.

Although slaves might become friendly with the master and his family, they still had to take orders. And if they committed crimes, they could be tortured, burned alive, crucified, or sent to fight wild beasts in the arena while the audience watched and cheered. The upper classes never suffered these violent punishments. Aristocratic criminals were killed with the sword—a quicker, less agonizing way to die.

Slaves were sometimes able to gain their freedom legally. Freedmen, as these lucky ones were called, were usually educated people or household workers. Freed slaves, both

Two strong slaves balance pottery jars on their shoulders and pour wine into cups held by other slaves. The cup bearers then serve the wine to their masters.

men and women, could legally marry—though a former slave could not marry a senator. They were even allowed to own property. Although freedmen could live anywhere they liked, many stayed with their former masters to work for pay. They still needed to make a living.

Even though slaves had few possessions of their own, Roman masters often gave gifts of money to hard workers. A slave could keep this gift, called a *peculium*, as his private property. Valuable slaves who were careful with their savings might eventually tuck away enough to buy their freedom. This system motivated slaves to work hard. It helped the masters too because, by the time a slave had saved enough money, he or she was probably growing old, and the master could use the money to buy another, younger, slave.

Many freedmen worked almost as hard as the slaves did. Most remained desperately poor. But at least as freedmen, they were servants who were paid for their work. And they could not be taken from their families and sold as Spartacus was.

CHAPTER 9

TWO REVOLUTIONARY BROTHERS

THE GRACCHI AND THE DECLINE OF THE REPUBLIC

Tiberius and Gaius Gracchus were two Roman brothers who fought and died for the same cause. They even died the same way, murdered in violent street brawls. But the two Gracchi were very different in age and personality. Plutarch, the Greek writer who brought so many Romans to life through his biographies, describes them: "Tiberius, in his looks . . . and gestures . . . was gentle and composed. But Gaius was fiery and passionate." When Tiberius gave a speech, he spoke quietly and never moved from one spot. But Gaius was like an actor. When he spoke to the people, he "would walk about, pacing on the platform. And in the heat of his orations, he would throw his cloak from his shoulders."

The Gracchi brothers were noblemen whose family was well known in Rome. Their father had served two terms as a consul, the highest office in Rome. Their mother, Cornelia, was the daughter of the general Scipio Africanus, who had defeated Rome's great enemy, the Carthaginian general Hannibal. (A king of Egypt once proposed marriage to Cornelia, but she turned him down.) As children of such distinguished parents, the Gracchi brothers had not only social rank but

In this life-size bronze statue, orator Aulus Metellus gives a speech. His short toga and high-laced shoes tell us that he is a Roman nobleman. His name is on the hem of his toga.

PLUTARCH AND SALLUST

Plutarch, *Life of Tiberius Gracchus,* 110 CE

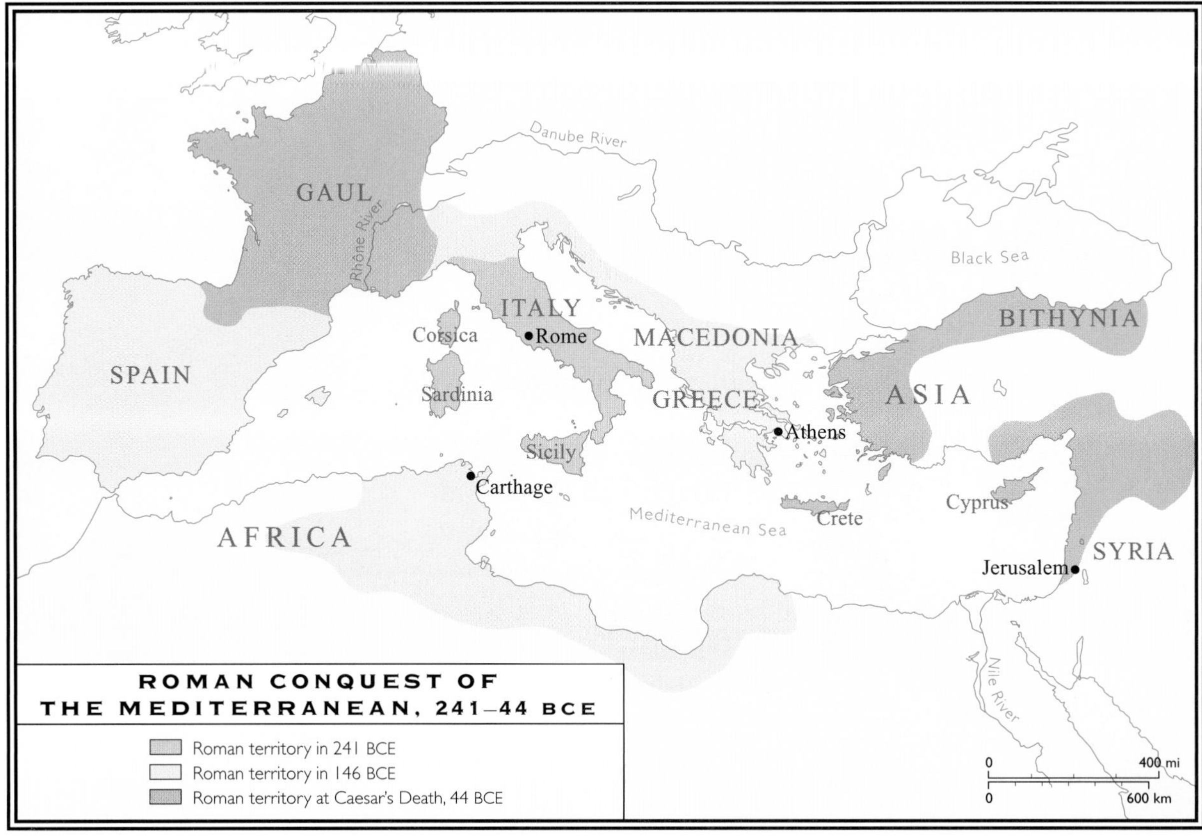

also plenty of money. Still, they devoted themselves to improving the lives of the poor.

Tiberius and Gaius entered politics in difficult times. The Roman Republic was in trouble. Like a teenager who grows tall "overnight," Rome had grown dramatically during the Punic Wars, from 264 to 146 BCE. And although 118 years is a long time for a person, it's a very short time for a city or empire. Rome entered the war years as a small city-state. It ended them as the ruler of the Mediterranean, controlling all of Italy, with conquered lands stretching from Africa and Spain to Greece. The once-poor farming community had mushroomed into a giant whose military conquests poured masses of gold, grain, and slaves into Italy.

Rome was suddenly rich and powerful. But it was also suddenly full of problems. Thousands of unemployed men hung around on the streets of the city, hoping to find work.

Many had lost their jobs to foreign slaves, who didn't have to be paid for their labor. Others in the street crowds were poor farmers whose land had been bought by wealthy aristocrats. These men could no longer farm. They couldn't join the army, either—only men who owned land could become soldiers. So what could they do? How could they feed themselves and their families?

Rome's elected officials didn't do much to improve the situation. More and more, they concentrated on what would be best for them instead of thinking about the common good. Instead of asking how they could help Rome and its people, they looked for ways to gain money and **importance** for themselves. Many fought their way to the top through bribery and corruption. Writing in the first century BCE, Sallust—a historian and a senator—describes his country's crisis: "Our country had grown great through hard work and the practice of justice . . . but then greed destroyed honor, integrity, and all other noble qualities; and in their place came . . . cruelty, neglect of the gods, and a belief that everything has a price."

"Important" and "importance" come from the Latin word *importare,* which means to bring in. Imagine a messenger, running to *bring in* urgent news of a victory on the battlefield or word of an illness, death, or birth.

Sallust, *Catiline,* 42 BCE

The army became unruly. Rebellious mobs roamed the city. Yet the Senate ignored these problems and tried to govern the sprawling empire as if it were still a small city-state. Rome's leaders seemed to be asking for trouble, and they got it. Trouble's name was Tiberius Gracchus, the older of the two Gracchi brothers.

Tiberius was elected a tribune of the people in 133 BCE. This office was first established to protect the plebeians, but later tribunes used it to advance their own careers. And as soon as Tiberius took office, he set to work for the rights of the plebs. The aristocrats in the Senate claimed that he was interested only in his own glory, but Tiberius denied it. He said that a trip through northern Italy had showed him how desperate the peasants really were. "The men who fight and die for Italy have only air and light. Without house or home, they wander with their wives and children in the open air. . . . They fight and die for the luxury and riches of others." Tiberius insisted that Rome should give the land it gained through war to the poor. Conquered territory

Plutarch, *Life of Tiberius Gracchus,* 110 CE

became state land. Technically, it belonged to Rome, but if wealthy citizens paid a small tax, they were allowed to farm it as their own. In this way most of the conquered territory passed into the hands of those who needed it least—the rich. Some aristocrats, including many senators, got tens of thousands of acres in this way. They used slave labor to work the land and made huge profits.

Tiberius made up his mind to change this law. He proposed that no one—no matter who his ancestors were—should be allowed to keep more than 300 acres of state land. The rest should be given to the poor. Once the homeless had land, he reasoned, they would be able to support themselves. They would no longer roam the cities in angry, hungry mobs. And, as landowners, they would be eligible to serve in the army. This would help the people, help the army, and help Rome—a "win" for everyone. But most of the senators stood against Tiberius, and it's easy to see why. His proposed law would rob them of the huge profits that they had enjoyed for so long.

Knowing that he had very little support among the senators, Tiberius bypassed the Senate and took his proposal directly to the Assembly of the Plebs. He needed votes for his plan to become law, so he arranged for peasants to be brought in from the countryside to increase the number of votes in his favor. When another tribune, Octavius, tried to use his veto to stop the vote, Tiberius called for the Assembly to throw him out. According to Plutarch, one of Tiberius's servants dragged Octavius away. Luckily for Octavius, his rich pals rescued him from the angry mob.

With Octavius out of the way, the Assembly voted Tiberius's proposal into law. The senators tried desperately to block the actual transfer of land. They knew that it would involve a mass of paperwork, which is always expensive. All of the new farmers would need animals and tools. The total cost would be enormous. So the Senate refused to cover expenses. That way, the hated law would be harmless—like a tiger without teeth. But Tiberius outsmarted them. He arranged to pay for the land transfers using money from a foreign kingdom.

Opinion in Rome was split. The *way* Tiberius had fought for his land reform, as much as the law itself, **infuriated** the senators. Tiberius had ignored the fact that the Senate was supposed to control Rome's finances. No wonder the noblemen hated him! But he became the common people's hero. This really worried the senators. They didn't want anyone to become too popular, especially with the plebs. When Tiberius began to walk through Rome accompanied by bodyguards, the senators feared the worst. They thought he planned to take over the government by force and rule on his own, tossing aside written laws and crippling the Senate's power.

furia = "rage"
"Infuriate" means to cause fury—to make someone angry.

No Roman official could be brought to trial while still in office. Tiberius's enemies planned to attack him as soon as his term ended. But he shocked them by announcing his plan to run for re-election. This wasn't supposed to happen. Tribunes were supposed to serve for one year only. Many aristocrats believed that the plebs would soon proclaim Tiberius king. Would a tyrant once again rule Rome?

A brawl broke out in the election assembly and Tiberius was killed in the street fighting that followed. For the first time in centuries, violence had entered Roman politics, and there it stayed until the fall of the Republic.

Tiberius had challenged the power of the Senate and won—even though he died in the process. His land reform had become law. A committee soon set to work distributing state-owned lands to the poor. Tiberius's brother Gaius was a member of that committee. In 123 BCE—ten years after Tiberius's death—Gaius followed in his brother's footsteps and was elected tribune.

Gaius was a true **revolutionary**, even more than Tiberius had been. The younger Gracchus was a great orator, and he pushed through some important reforms. His grain law, for example, kept the price of grain low enough that ordinary citizens could afford to buy bread for their families.

"Revolutionary" comes from the word *revolvere,* which means to revolve, to turn or roll back. The revolutionary Gracchi brothers tried to turn things around . . . turn the world upside down.

Like his brother, Gaius fought against the power of the nobles. He changed the jury system so that when senators were tried in the courts for corruption, the jury would include some men who weren't members of the Senate. This change made it harder for corrupt senators to get away with their crimes. Although Gaius was re-elected, opposition to him grew among Rome's nobility. And like Tiberius, Gaius met his death in a street battle during his second term in office.

Gaius had fought for the rights of Rome's Italian allies, saying that they deserved citizenship. The allies agreed. They had helped Rome to conquer the Mediterranean and yet they didn't have the rights that Roman citizens enjoyed. In 90 BCE, more than thirty years after Gaius's death, Rome's Italian allies rebelled. (This revolution is usually called the Social War, but its other name, the War of the Allies, describes it better.) The non-Roman Italians established their own capital and issued coins showing the Italian bull goring the Roman wolf. The war came to an end when Rome granted citizenship to all free, male inhabitants of Italy.

Gaius Gracchus meets his death in this 18th-century painting. There was no police force to control the mobs who fought in the streets of Rome.

Although the Gracchi brothers had made some progress toward their goals, neither had solved the problems of the poor. Much of the distributed land was soon bought up by the wealthy. The poor lost ground, sliding back to where they had been before the reforms. When the Gracchi's reforms failed, the poor people of Rome became even more dissatisfied. It was as though the taste of hope had made them impatient for the feast they believed should be theirs. In the years that followed the deaths of the Gracchi, a new group of politicians appeared in Rome: the ***populares***. Like Tiberius and Gaius, the *populares* spoke for the common people. These politicians played an important role in the conflicts that ended the Roman Republic.

populus = "people"
The *populares* were politicians who championed the common folk of Rome—the *populus Romanus*.

CHAPTER 10

APPIAN, CICERO, AND PLUTARCH

WORDS VERSUS SWORDS

CICERO AND THE CRISIS OF THE REPUBLIC

Everyone in first-century BCE Rome knew Marcus Tullius Cicero's name. He served as a consul—Rome's top office—and his fiery speeches drew crowds of listeners. When Cato the Younger, the great grandson of Cato the Censor, called Cicero "the father of his country," everyone cheered. Yet Cicero's letters show that he sometimes couldn't decide what to do. And he worried a lot about his children. When his daughter Tullia died, he was heartbroken. He wrote to his best friend, Atticus, about his sadness:

Appian, *Civil Wars,* 160 CE

Cicero, *Letters to Atticus,* 45 BCE

> I have isolated myself, in this lonely region. . . . In the morning, I hide myself in the dense . . . forest and don't come out until night. . . . My only form of communication now is through books, but even my reading is interrupted by fits of crying.

Cicero wrote hundreds, maybe thousands, of letters. Amazingly, 900 of them have survived, more than 2,000 years later. They include letters to his friends and to other politicians, in addition to those that he wrote to his brother and his unruly, playboy son. In them, we learn about family problems, deaths, and divorces—not to mention his opinions on almost everything.

Like many grown-ups, Cicero liked to give advice, and his letters are generously sprinkled with hints, warnings, and words of wisdom. He was often pompous, even conceited, but he showed his feelings in his writing, even when his honesty made him seem weak or afraid.

Some of Cicero's letters report on the latest happenings in Rome. His words give us the best picture we have of life in the 1st century BCE. He wrote about simple things: the weather, gladiatorial games, and the price of bread. But he also described wars, riots, scandals, and the plots of scheming politicians.

Many of Cicero's speeches and essays have also survived. They tell us what he thought about friendship, education, law, patriotism, and loyalty—to name a few of his topics. In an essay on duty, he described what a gentleman should and should not do. According to Cicero, it was just fine for a gentleman to own a farm, but he mustn't do the actual digging, planting, or plowing himself. In fact, a true gentleman would *never* work with his hands.

Cicero was a snob. He looked down on workers—even shopkeepers. He said that "they couldn't make a profit unless they lied a lot. And nothing is more shameful than lying." He disdained fishermen, butchers, cooks, poultry sellers, perfume makers, and dancers because their work appealed to the senses of taste, sight, and smell. What would he say about hairdressers, movie stars, and rock stars if he were alive today?

" Cicero, *An Essay about Duties*, 44 BCE

Cicero was born in 106 BCE in the small town of Arpinum, not far from Rome. He came from a wealthy family that was

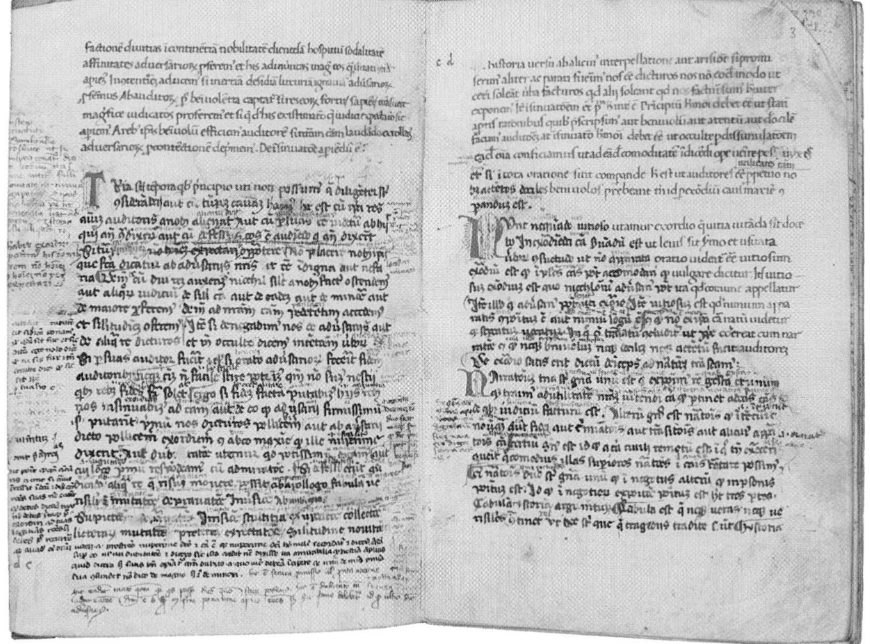

This copy of Cicero's handbook, Rhetorica ad Herennium *(dedicated to Herennius), comes from 15th-century Italy. Educated people were still writing in Latin, copying Cicero's style.*

"Words cannot express . . . how bitterly we are hated among foreign nations because of the . . . outrageous conduct of the men whom we have sent to govern them."

Cicero, Roman orator, ***On the Manilian Law,* 66 BCE**

well known in the region. But because none of his ancestors had ever served in the Roman Senate, Cicero was considered a "new man"—an outsider, not a genuine aristocrat.

As a teenager, Cicero traveled and studied in Greece, North Africa, and Asia. While in Athens, he began his training as an orator—a skilled public speaker—convinced that this would be important in his political career. He was right. He understood that an orator needs a good memory and a huge store of information. But he said that it wasn't enough just to spout off a string of facts. An orator should use an actor's skills to put across his ideas. The words of a speech, "must be reinforced by bodily movement, gesture, facial expression, and by changes in the voice itself."

“ Cicero, *On the Orator,* 55 BCE

When the aspiring young politician finished his travels, he settled in Rome. Although he hated the corruption that he saw among the city's officials, he wanted to join their club. He hoped to become a magistrate and convince the others to govern once again with honor and justice—to forget their own ambitions and work for the common good.

Cicero wasn't a coward. He never hesitated to point out the crimes that he saw, even if high-ranking officials had committed them. His first legal case pitted him against a top lawyer. Against all odds, he won. This victory made his reputation as the young man who beat an old pro.

In 75 BCE the people elected Cicero quaestor, an assistant to the governor of Sicily, when he was 30 years old—the youngest age the law allowed. Even though his ancestors had never held major office in Rome, Cicero climbed the ladder of success very quickly. He did it through hard work and **innate** brilliance. But Rome was like a boiling pot of trouble in Cicero's day, just as it had been when the Gracchi brothers were alive. Fierce battles still raged in the streets because so many people were hungry and jobless.

"Innate" comes from the word *innatus*, which means "born in." An innate skill is not something you learn; you're born with it. Cicero's determination was an innate trait—he was born that way!

Riots and corruption had threatened Rome's security in the age of the Gracchi. Afterward, the situation grew even worse. German tribes moved south into Roman territory in southern Gaul (modern France), where they defeated Roman armies in three frightening battles. This was the first time since Hannibal that foreign invaders had threatened Italy. Faced with new enemies, Rome desperately recruited soldiers. The consul Gaius Marius enlisted a new army, even accepting poor men who owned no land. Although soldiers usually supplied their own equipment, Marius gave uniforms and weapons to these new recruits.

Marius defeated the foreign invaders, but the victory turned into a disaster for the Republic. Men who had once roamed the city in angry mobs now eagerly joined the army. There, they would be fed and paid. And they knew that after the war was over, their generals would give them a reward of land or money. No wonder the soldiers felt a greater loyalty to their generals than to the Roman state that had failed them! Ruthless generals took advantage of the situation. They led their armies against one another, each hoping to gain control of the city. These **civil** wars rocked the Republic again and again.

"Civil" comes from the word *civis*, which means citizen. A civil war is fought between the citizens of a single country, such as the wars that raged in Rome in the final decades of the Republic.

Cicero was determined to save the Roman Republic. He gathered strong allies, especially men who could recruit soldiers. One of the men whom he enlisted in the cause was Pompey, a powerful general. Pompey and Cicero had been friends since they were both 17 years old, and they had helped each other over the years. Cicero's orations in the Forum helped Pompey to gain support for his military ambitions. After Cicero spoke on Pompey's behalf, the Assembly gave Pompey a fleet of 500 ships and an army of 125,000 men to command against the pirates who threatened Rome in the eastern Mediterranean. He was victorious within a few months and became Rome's leading commander—thanks to Cicero's speech.

When Cicero was elected consul in 63 BCE, he was conceited enough to believe that his consulship would be the turning point for the ailing Republic. Could its troubles all be over? He thought so. Once elected, he opposed the *populares,* who supported the reforms of the Gracchi brothers. He spoke for the aristocrats in the Senate and tried to create an alliance of the rich—nobles and businessmen—against the poor. One *popularis* politician, Lucius Catiline, organized a rebellion. Cicero squelched it and executed the rebel leaders without a trial. He later paid a high price for his actions. His enemies watched and waited. In the end, Cicero's old friend Pompey deserted him and made new alliances. Cicero told him: "You have given us a strong hope of peace. We have this good news because of you. And I've told everyone so. But I must warn you that your old enemies are now posing as your friends."

“ Cicero, *Letters to his Friends,* 62 BCE

tres + *vir* = "three" + "men" A triumvirate is a council of three people. Although the First Triumvirate was really a private political deal, the Romans had other triumvirates such as the "Board of Three" that carried out public executions.

Pompey paid no attention to Cicero's words. By 60 BCE, he had teamed up with the *popularis* politician Julius Caesar and the millionaire Crassus. The three formed a **triumvirate** and shared the power among themselves. Together, they controlled the Senate, the people . . . Rome itself. Many Romans, including Cicero, were shocked to learn of it. But, arrogant as ever, Cicero refused to cooperate with this First Triumvirate. He called it "a three-headed monster." Now Cicero's longtime enemies saw their chance, and they persuaded the Assembly to banish Cicero from Rome. Later Pompey intervened on his behalf, and Cicero was called back in 57 BCE.

Cicero stayed loyal to Pompey and fought at his side when a civil war broke out between Pompey and Caesar. Caesar won and became the most powerful man in Rome. After Pompey's death, Caesar pardoned Cicero and allowed him to return to his beloved Rome.

A few years later Cicero landed in trouble once again. By this time, all three members of the Triumvirate were dead, and Mark Antony held the reins of power in Rome. Cicero, outspoken as usual and still fighting to save the Republic, delivered passionate speeches against Antony. He spoke, privately and publicly, against him. He begged Antony to put the good of the Republic above his own desires. He used his own record to try to convince Antony: "I defended the Republic as a young man. I will not abandon it now that I am old. . . . Nor will I tremble before your sword. No, I would cheerfully offer myself to its blade, if the liberty of the city could be restored by my death."

Cicero, *Second Philippic,* 43 BCE

Mark Antony was not impressed by Cicero's brave, unselfish words. Instead, Antony convinced his ally, Caesar's great-nephew Octavian, that Cicero was a threat and should be killed. Antony's soldiers tracked down the aging orator at his seaside villa and murdered him. Then, in an act of terrible cruelty, the general gave orders for Cicero's head and hands to be cut off and displayed in the Forum where he had so often spoken.

Cicero's voice was silenced, and yet his writings remained. He is honored today as a man of genius and a master of words. He was both. Perhaps he was in the right place at the wrong time. Generals, not orators, ruled Rome in the 1st century BCE.

A teacher, surrounded by his students, reads from a scroll made from papyrus reeds from Egypt. Like other Greek and Roman writers, Cicero wrote his books on papyrus.

During his own lifetime, Cicero was known as a great statesman, orator, and man of action. But he died a bitterly disappointed man. He had failed to do what he most wanted to accomplish: to save the Roman Republic. Not even Cicero's enemies, though, could doubt his love for Rome. Plutarch, writing many years after Cicero's death, tells a story about Octavian—after he had risen to great power as the emperor Augustus Caesar. The emperor found his grandson reading a book written by Cicero. Knowing that his grandfather had agreed to let Mark Antony's soldiers murder Cicero, "The boy was afraid and tried to hide it under his gown. Augustus . . . took the book from him, and began to read it. . . . When he gave it back to his grandson, he said, 'My child, this was a learned man, and a lover of his country.'"

Plutarch, *Life of Cicero,* 110 CE

CHAPTER 11

COIN STRUCK BY MARCUS METTIUS, PLUTARCH, AND SUETONIUS

"I CAME, I SAW, I CONQUERED"

JULIUS CAESAR AND THE ROMAN TRIUMPH

Coin of Caesar struck by Marcus Mettius, 44 BCE

In February of 44 BCE, the Roman Senate declared Julius Caesar dictator of Rome for life. According to the Greek writer Plutarch, the Senate also offered Caesar a crown, but he turned it down. Caesar knew how much Romans had hated the idea of kings since the reign of Tarquin the Proud, 500 years before.

One month later, Julius Caesar was dead, murdered in the Senate. Why? This ancient coin may provide the answer.

On it, we see the face of Julius Caesar, a thin, handsome man with fine features, the perfect image of a noble Roman. Caesar himself had ordered the coin to be made, so it probably looks very much like him. He was the first living Roman to be depicted on a coin—by tradition, leaders and heroes received this honor only after their deaths. On the dictator's head is a laurel wreath, a symbol of victory. When Caesar's enemies saw this coin, they began to question his plans. Did he intend to become Rome's king after all? Did he plan to set up a monarchy with his children and grandchildren ruling after him? This fear haunted many senators as they watched Caesar's power and popularity grow.

Soon after the coin appeared, a group of senators met to plot his murder.

In early March, people reported bizarre happenings: strange birds seen in the Forum and odd sounds heard there. Then, when Caesar was sacrificing to the gods, one of the animals was found to have no heart! Many believed that these happenings were omens—warnings of disasters to come.

On March 15, the day known in Rome as the Ides of March, Caesar went to a meeting of the Senate. As usual, he had no bodyguards. On the way, a soothsayer—a "truth teller" who can tell the future—stopped him with a warning: "Caesar, beware the Ides of March." (The Romans called the middle day of the month the "Ides"; it usually fell on the 15th.) The dictator ignored him and walked on. But when he arrived at the meeting place, a group of senators—mostly old friends and men he had pardoned and promoted—surrounded him. They quickly closed in and, drawing their knives, began to stab him. Bleeding from 23 brutal wounds, Caesar fell and died at the base of a statue he had commissioned: a statue of Pompey—his rival and friend.

Plutarch, *Life of Caesar,* 110 CE

Who was this man who stirred such a powerful mix of love, admiration, fear, and hatred?

Julius Caesar was born into a noble family, but he always supported the rights of the common people. He was the plebeians' favorite politician. They believed that he understood and cared about their needs. He did, but he was no saint. He was practical, strong willed, and hungry for power. Street-smart, he made very few mistakes, and he knew how to take advantage of the mistakes of his enemies.

In 60 BCE, Julius Caesar wanted to become a consul, but he was broke. He had already spent everything he had (or could borrow) to pay for his political career up to that point. He needed money and he needed help. So he made a bargain with two other men who also needed something: Cicero's friend Pompey and Crassus, the richest man in Rome. The three formed the First Triumvirate.

The Triumvirate was a political deal. Each member gained something from it. Crassus had arranged for his wealthy friends to collect taxes in the provinces—Rome's possessions beyond the Italian peninsula. This was a profitable position because tax collectors kept some of the money for themselves. Joining the alliance of power let Crassus protect these moneymaking deals. Pompey joined to make sure that his soldiers stayed loyal to him. As a member of the Triumvirate, he could guarantee that they would be rewarded for their service.

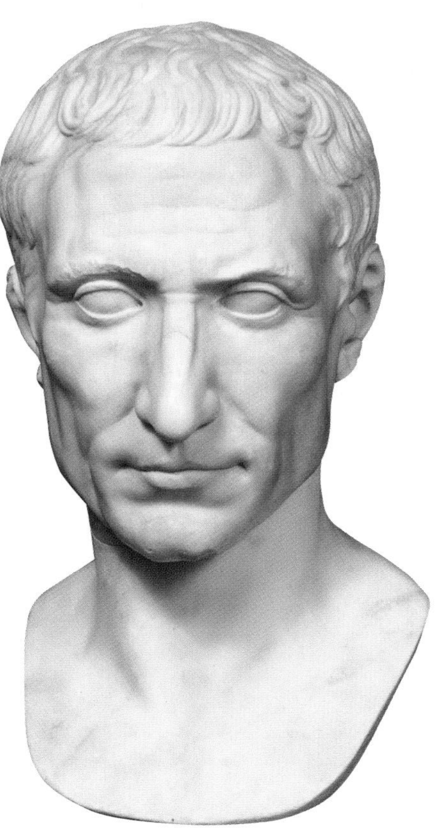

In this bust, sculpted late in his life, Julius Caesar has hair. But other pictures show that he was bald by then.

Caesar got what he wanted, too. He not only became consul, but the next year he became governor of Gaul (France), a province about the size of Texas. There, Caesar established himself as a major power. He spent almost ten years conquering Gaul, pitting his loyal, well-trained army against the Gauls, who were mostly independent tribes fighting among themselves. Beginning in 58 BCE, Caesar and his troops moved through the region and overcame it, bit by bit. In the process, Rome built roads, captured over a million prisoners, and took huge amounts of money and treasure from the native peoples.

Caesar's success in Gaul made him rich and even more ambitious. This worried his rivals and enemies in Rome. They knew that he favored the Gracchi brothers' plan for taking land from the rich and giving it to the poor. This made him even less popular with the aristocrats.

"Military" comes from the Latin word for soldier, *miles*. If a person is militant, he or she behaves like a soldier and is ready to fight.

By 50 BCE, the Triumvirate had ended. Crassus had been killed in battle, and Pompey had become very jealous of Caesar's **military** success and his great popularity. Pompey had married Caesar's daughter, Julia, but when she died in childbirth, the bond between the two men was broken. Before Caesar returned from Gaul, Pompey sided with the Senate to declare his former father-in-law an enemy of the State. The Senate demanded that Caesar give up his army and return to Rome. Knowing that he would be arrested if he obeyed, he refused. But now his life and career were at stake. Did he dare go back to Italy at all?

In January of 49 BCE, Caesar's forces were camped just north of the Rubicon, the river that marked the boundary between Gaul and Italy. As soon as Caesar heard the Senate's ruling, he slipped away from the camp with a few trusted men. It was night, and everyone else was feasting. No one noticed that he was missing. When he reached the banks of the Rubicon, he paused, thinking about his next step. After a moment, he declared, "The die is cast" and crossed the river. This was his way of saying that his mind was made up and wouldn't be changed. Now he was ready to meet his former ally, the great general Pompey, in battle.

“ Suetonius, *Life of the Deified Julius*, 130 CE

Caesar was never one to stand around, waiting for someone else to do something. Decisive as always, he began his march right away. He set out in the dead of winter with a single legion of soldiers. He knew that by marching on Rome he would start a civil war. What he didn't know—and couldn't have known—was that this war would last for nearly two decades and destroy the Republic.

Pompey would have liked more time to train his troops; they were not as battle-ready as Caesar's army. When Caesar's troops entered Italy, Pompey's soldiers panicked and many deserted. Pompey gathered what troops he could and escaped from Rome just before Caesar arrived. Caesar had Pompey on the run.

Caesar entered Rome for the first time in nine years. He found the government in chaos. Again, he didn't hold back but set to work right away. He asked the Senate to join forces with him to avoid more bloodshed. He chose Mark Antony as his chief lieutenant—next in command. Then, delegating power to other trusted generals, Caesar himself set out for Greece. There he defeated Pompey's army in 48 BCE.

This solid, rectangular building normally housed the Senate's meetings. But because it was closed for repairs, the Senators gathered in the Theater of Pompey on the Ides of March, 44 BCE.

MATH, ROMAN STYLE

Roman numbers were written in two ways: in words and symbols. We do the same. We can write "one" or its numeral, 1. The Romans wrote *unus* or its numeral, I. Two (*duo*) = II. Three (*tres*) = III. Four (*quattuor*) = IV. Five (*quintus*) = V. Six (*sextus*) = VI. Seven (*septem*) = VII. Eight (*octo*) = VIII. Nine (*novem*) = IX. Ten (*decem*) = X.

Roman numerals are easy to figure out once you understand the system. One, two, and three are like marks in the sand, but four (IV) is written to show that it is one less than five (V). Nine (IX) is the same. It's one less than ten (X) and eleven (XI) is one more than ten. Any numeral written before a bigger one means, "subtract." Written after, it means, "add."

Plutarch, *Life of Caesar,* 110 CE

Plutarch reports that when Caesar saw the dead Romans lying on the field, he groaned and said: "They made this happen; they drove me to it."

News of Caesar's victory was greeted back home with wild excitement. His popularity soared, and Rome elected him to a second consulship.

Meanwhile Pompey had escaped to Egypt, arriving in the midst of a civil war between 15-year-old King Ptolemy XIII and his older sister, Cleopatra VII. Ptolemy believed that Caesar would follow his rival to Egypt, and he was right. So he prepared a surprise for the general. Hoping to please Caesar and lure him to his side against Cleopatra, Ptolemy's advisors captured Pompey and cut off his head. Then they pickled it in brine. They expected Caesar to be delighted, but they were wrong.

When Caesar arrived in Egypt, Ptolemy presented Caesar with Pompey's pickled head—the head of the noble Roman who had been his rival but also his friend and former son-in-law. Disgusted and pained, Caesar turned away and wept. He commanded that Pompey's body be buried with honor. And he ordered the execution of the Egyptians who had murdered a great leader of the Roman people.

WHAT WAS IT WORTH?

The basic Roman coin was the silver *denarius*—worth about a day's pay for an ordinary laborer. Everyday purchases were made with less valuable coins made of bronze. Gold coins were rare and were equal to 25 silver *denarii*. Caesar's gift of 100 *denarii* (the plural of *denarius*) was a huge amount of money, almost half a year's pay for an ordinary laborer.

Caesar then restored Cleopatra to her throne and defeated her brother in battle. On his way back to Rome, Caesar passed through Asia. There, he squashed a rebellion in Asia Minor (modern Turkey). In a letter to a friend, he made light of the victory. The letter had only three words: "*Veni, vidi, vici.*" ("I came, I saw, I conquered.") Plutarch says that this brief message matched "the sharpness and speed of the battle itself." Caesar's fans later made placards with these three words written on them, which they carried in his triumphal procession into Rome.

Plutarch, *Life of Caesar,* 110 CE

When Caesar returned to Rome, he was proclaimed dictator. Then he began the work of healing Rome's terrible war wounds. He gave 100 *denarii* to every citizen and pardoned his own enemies, even those who had supported Pompey against him, including Cicero and Brutus. (Caesar was especially fond of Brutus. In his youth, Caesar had been in love with Brutus's mother, and he always looked out for her son. Brutus did not return the favor.)

During four years of almost absolute power, Caesar passed many laws to control debt, reduce unemployment, and regulate traffic in Rome. He levied taxes on foreign imports to boost Rome's economy. He put unemployed Romans to work building a new Forum and a large public building named in his family's honor: the Basilica Julia. He planned the first public library and built embankments along the Tiber to protect the city against floods. He revised the old Roman calendar, replacing it with the one that we use today, beginning with January.

Julius Caesar was perhaps the most extraordinary of all ancient Romans—a senator, military leader, and dictator of Rome. But he was also a poet, a brilliant historian who wrote about his military victories, and the only orator of his day who could compete with Cicero. His personal charm brought him the loyalty of men and the love of women.

Caesar's body, covered by his toga, lies at the feet of Pompey's statue in this 19th-century painting. With their arms and daggers held high, his assassins celebrate their victory.

In the end, he was killed at the height of his powers by men he thought were his friends. It was particularly sad that Brutus was among the assassins. According to Suetonius, Caesar, as he was dying, turned to Brutus and said, "You too, my son?"

Suetonius, *Life of the Deified Julius,* 130 CE

Brutus didn't feel guilty about betraying Caesar. He was proud of it. His ancestor was the Brutus who had expelled the last king, Tarquin the Proud, from Rome. Brutus issued a coin to celebrate the Ides of March as Caesar's assassination day. The coin shows the deadly daggers that had killed Caesar and the "cap of liberty" traditionally worn by slaves after they were freed. Brutus bragged that he had saved Rome from slavery.

But the murder of Julius Caesar did Rome no good. The city faced another 13 years of civil unrest and war. Assassination *did* help Caesar's reputation, though. In his will, Caesar left a gift of money to every Roman citizen. More than ever, he was the common man's hero, so admired that later rulers of Rome adopted the name Caesar.

Brutus and his friends thought they were serving Rome and saving the Republic by killing a man who had become too powerful, a man they feared might make himself king. They were shortsighted. The Republic was already dying . . . almost dead. Rome would soon be dominated by a single ruler. That man would be Caesar's great-nephew and heir, Augustus Caesar.

CHAPTER 12

POWER-MAD OR MADLY IN LOVE?

CLEOPATRA, QUEEN OF EGYPT

PLUTARCH

Ptolemy XII was pharaoh of Egypt, the wealthiest country in the Mediterranean world. Ptolemy loved to party—he was called "The Flute Player" because he was so fond of music. But Ptolemy was not just a playful fellow. He was also a troublesome one, so troublesome that his own people wanted him out. They booted him from power in 58 BCE and put his eldest daughter, Berenice, on the throne instead.

Ptolemy fought back. He traveled to Rome and bribed the general Pompey to support him against Berenice. Pompey took troops to Egypt, defeated Berenice's supporters, and returned the playboy king to his throne. In gratitude, Ptolemy named Pompey as legal guardian to his eldest son. Ptolemy then gave orders for Berenice to be beheaded.

Who was this man who ordered his own daughter's death?

Ptolemy XII was actually a Greek. His long-ago ancestor, the first Ptolemy, had served as a general under Alexander the Great, who, in 331 BCE, had conquered a huge empire—including Egypt. When Alexander died, his three top generals divided the empire among themselves. The one who chose Egypt made himself its king and called himself Ptolemy I. By the time Ptolemy XII came to the throne, his family had ruled Egypt for almost 250 years. But they still spoke Greek and considered themselves part of the Greek world.

Cleopatra may not have been drop-dead gorgeous, but her personality must have sizzled—she was loved by two of Rome's most powerful men: Julius Caesar and Mark Antony.

Although Ptolemy had executed his eldest daughter, there was another whom he especially loved—a bright, lively girl named Cleopatra VII. The king seems to have found her the most interesting of all his children. He proclaimed her a goddess when she was about four years old.

Cleopatra went to the palace school with the other royal princes and princesses. She became fluent in nine languages and was the first member of her family who could speak Egyptian. Cleopatra had tremendous appeal. Even the Greek biographer Plutarch, who disapproved of her behavior, describes her in glowing terms: "The charm of her presence was irresistible, but there was an attraction in her person and conversation, together with a force of character, which showed in her every word and action. Everyone who met her fell under her spell."

“ Plutarch, *Life of Antony*, 110 CE

When Ptolemy died in 51 BCE, he left his kingdom to the 18-year-old Cleopatra. Even though she was old enough to rule, according to Egyptian law, she couldn't rule alone. Ptolemy's will set up joint rule by Cleopatra and her 12-year-old brother, Ptolemy XIII.

Consors = "partner" or "neighbor" "Consort" can simply mean "companion," but it is often used as the name of a ruler's husband or wife. Great Britain's Queen Victoria was married to Prince Albert. He was a prince and the royal consort, but never a king.

According to Egyptian tradition, pharaohs married their siblings or children to keep power within the royal family. Cleopatra had to marry a brother or a son, and this **consort** would be her official husband. It would be a marriage of politics, not love. Cleopatra had no sons when she came to the throne, so her first co-ruler was Ptolemy XIII.

Cleopatra and Ptolemy ruled together for several years, but Cleopatra wasn't very good at sharing. She left her brother's name out of official documents—on purpose—and had her own picture and name stamped on Egyptian coins. This didn't go over very well with Ptolemy. Nor did it please the court officials of Alexandria, the capital city.

Alexandria's officials decided that Ptolemy would be easier to control than Cleopatra. So they plotted to overthrow the strong-willed queen. Knowing that her life was in danger, Cleopatra escaped to Syria, where she raised an army to help her regain power.

In 48 BCE, while Cleopatra was away, Pompey came back to Egypt, this time fleeing from Julius Caesar. Since Pompey was Ptolemy's legal guardian, the general thought that he could count on the young king of Egypt to protect him. Instead, Ptolemy allowed his advisors to murder and behead the Roman general.

Caesar arrived in Alexandria four days later with 3,200 foot soldiers and 800 cavalrymen. After having Pompey's murderers executed, Caesar took over the royal palace and immediately began giving orders. This news reached Cleopatra in Syria, and she realized that control of Egypt hung in the balance. If power was changing hands, she did not intend to miss out. She smuggled herself back into Alexandria, passing through enemy lines rolled up in a carpet. She was delivered—in the carpet—to Caesar. Imagine his surprise when the carpet was unrolled, and there, before him, was the beautiful young queen of Egypt!

Caesar had summoned both Ptolemy and Cleopatra to appear before him. The next morning, when Ptolemy arrived at the palace, he discovered that Cleopatra had gotten there first. It soon became clear to 15-year-old Ptolemy that Caesar and Cleopatra had formed a close alliance. They had, in fact, become lovers. Ptolemy could easily see that Caesar would support Cleopatra's claim to the throne, not his. Shouting that he had been betrayed, Ptolemy stormed out into the streets of Alexandria and started to organize a mob against his sister.

Ptolemy gathered an army of 20,000 men. His troops surrounded Caesar, but the great Roman overcame them with his own troops and executed their general. The boy-king drowned in the Nile River while trying to escape.

Ptolemy's death left Cleopatra alone on the throne, but only for a little while. She had to marry another brother in order to pacify the priests and government officials of Alexandria. This brother, her second consort, was also named Ptolemy—Ptolemy XIV.

Most historians agree that Caesar planned to place Cleopatra on the throne of Egypt. But scholars disagree about why. Was he in love with her? Or did he just believe that he could control her . . . that she would be a useful puppet-queen for Rome? No one knows.

When Caesar returned to Rome in 46 BCE, Cleopatra followed him. Even though he already had a wife, the dictator kept Cleopatra and their infant son, Caesarion, in another

THE GODDESS ISIS

Cleopatra often presented herself as the goddess Isis, the Egyptian goddess of fertility and harvest. On ceremonial occasions, she often wore black robes, imitating the traditional image of the goddess.

Mark Antony was Julius Caesar's chief deputy when he first met the ruler's mistress, Cleopatra. Eight years later, in 36 BCE, Caesar was dead and Antony married the Egyptian queen.

home. There, she lived in great luxury and, one way or another, managed to offend almost everyone in Rome.

The assassination of Caesar two years later left Cleopatra in danger. She knew that no one in Rome would defend her, so she sailed back to Alexandria, taking Caesarion with her. Once there, she arranged for her brother, Ptolemy XIV, to be assassinated. She made young Caesarion her new co-ruler.

Cleopatra found Egypt in a bad state, weakened by drought and years of poor harvests. The people were hungry, but the royal treasury was nearly empty. Cleopatra knew that she must connect herself to a source of power. And power, in 41 BCE, meant Rome. So when Mark Antony invited her to meet him in Tarsus (an ancient city in what is now Turkey), she accepted. Even though her country was teetering on the edge of financial collapse, she put on an extravagant show to impress and woo him. Plutarch describes how she

Plutarch, *Life of Antony*, 110 CE

> sailed up the . . . river in a flat-bottomed boat . . . with its purple sails outstretched, pulled by silver oars. . . . She herself reclined under a gold-embroidered awning, dressed like Venus. . . . Her slaves, dressed as cupids, fanned her on each side.

Antony was married, but he fell for Cleopatra like a fish taking the bait. He spent the winter with her in Alexandria. It seemed that she could get anything she wanted from him. He even began to wear Eastern clothes instead of the traditional Roman toga. Sometimes, for fun, Antony and Cleopatra dressed as slaves or servants and roamed the streets playing pranks on anyone they met. According to Plutarch, the people of Alexandria were charmed at the sight of a Roman general behaving in such a silly way. "The Alexandrians . . . enjoyed taking part in these amusements. . . . They liked Antony personally and used to say that he put on his tragic mask for the Romans, but kept the comic one for them."

Plutarch, *Life of Antony*, 110 CE

Meanwhile, Caesar's heir, Octavian was still in Rome. He and Antony had been partners. They had defeated and killed Caesar's assassins and were now supposedly ruling the empire together. But when Antony's wife became involved in a civil war against Octavian, Antony had to leave Cleopatra and return to Rome to deal with the crisis. His wife became ill and died, leaving Antony free to marry again. He could have chosen Cleopatra, but he made a political marriage instead. He married Octavian's sister, Octavia—a beautiful, intelligent widow. She and Antony had a daughter. Back in Egypt, though, Cleopatra had already given birth to Antony's children, a twin boy and girl.

Even though Octavia was expecting their second child, Mark Antony suddenly went back to Alexandria . . . and Cleopatra, whom he married under Egyptian law. Octavian was furious. His sister had been rejected and shamed. He declared war against Antony and Cleopatra.

In 31 BCE, Octavian's navy defeated Mark Antony in Greece. Morale sank among Antony's troops. Many soldiers deserted and joined Octavian. Supplies of food and water

In the 1963 movie Cleopatra, *Elizabeth Taylor played Cleopatra and Richard Burton played Mark Antony. The ancient story cast its spell: the stars, Taylor and Burton, fell in love and later married.*

grew scarce for Antony's army. His forces suffered a fatal blow when Octavian crushed them in the Battle of Actium, a city on the western coast of Greece. Cleopatra, seeing the disaster from a distance, ordered her ships to return to Egypt. Antony saw her purple sails in retreat and ordered his sailors to follow. But Antony's ground forces continued to fight. They couldn't believe at first that their beloved leader had abandoned them. When they realized it was true, they simply laid down their weapons and surrendered.

Cleopatra and her servants escape in a small boat, leaving her lover, Mark Antony, to fight on alone against the more powerful Romans in the fierce Battle of Actium.

The final battle between Antony and Octavian began near Alexandria on the first of August, 30 BCE. Antony ordered his fleet to attack, and his men obediently rowed toward the enemy ships. Then, instead of attacking, they saluted the enemy's leader: Octavian. Antony's cavalry

deserted as well. Only the foot soldiers remained loyal to their general, but they were easily defeated.

Antony was infuriated that Cleopatra had ordered her troops to abandon the battle and return to Egypt. Plutarch writes that the defeated general "retreated into Alexandria, crying out in his rage that Cleopatra had betrayed him to the very men he had fought for her sake." Cleopatra, fearing her lover's anger, hid in a huge, two-story tomb and sent a servant to tell Antony that she was dead.

Plutarch, *Life of Antony*, 110 CE

When Antony heard the news, he was devastated. He said he had no reason to live. The war was lost and Cleopatra was dead. So he stabbed himself, by falling on his own sword. He was dying, but not yet dead, when Cleopatra's second messenger arrived, inviting Antony to come to her hiding place. The queen was alive after all. She had changed her mind and wanted to see Antony. But it was almost too late.

Antony commanded his slaves to lift him up. Plutarch says that they carried Antony to the tomb, but

> even then, Cleopatra would not allow the doors to be opened, but she showed herself at a window and let down cords and ropes to the ground. The slaves fastened Antony to these and the queen pulled him up. . . . Cleopatra . . . laid him upon a bed . . . and smeared her face with his blood. She called him her lord and husband and commander.

Plutarch, *Life of Antony*, 110 CE

Antony died in the arms of the queen.

With Antony dead and Cleopatra defeated, Octavian was the undisputed ruler of the known world. Cleopatra tried to make him fall in love with her. He could have been her third great Roman—but he wasn't interested. Instead, Octavian planned to take Cleopatra, the last Ptolemaic ruler of Egypt, to Rome as his slave.

Rather than be humiliated, Cleopatra chose death. She tried to kill herself, but Octavian's guards caught and stopped her. However, in the end she succeeded with a trick. The queen humbly asked the conqueror to allow her to mourn Antony's death and to give his body a proper farewell. Octavian agreed.

DEATH BY ASP

An asp is a small, Egyptian cobra. Because she had tested various poisons on condemned prisoners, Cleopatra knew that its poison worked quickly and didn't cause too much pain.

Cleopatra ordered a bath to be made ready and when she had bathed, she put on her royal robes and ate a fancy meal. Soon an Egyptian peasant arrived with a basket of figs. The guard inspected it but didn't see the asp, a poisonous snake, hidden beneath the fruit. Cleopatra sent away all of her servants except two women whom she especially trusted and loved. These servants locked the doors of the tomb, obeying the queen's command. Cleopatra had planned to let the asp come upon her when she wasn't looking. But according to one story by Plutarch, as soon as she saw the snake, she grabbed it and pressed it onto her bare arm, inviting a fatal bite.

When Octavian's messengers broke into the tomb, they found Cleopatra and one of her handmaidens already dead. The other servant was dying—like her mistress, poisoned by the asp. Octavian was angry to have lost his prize, but he admired the queen's courage and determination.

Plutarch writes that Octavian commanded that she be "buried with royal splendor and magnificence, and her body laid beside Antony's." He then gave orders for Caesarion's execution. For Octavian, the great Julius Caesar could have only one heir—himself.

“ Plutarch, *Life of Antony*, 110 CE

What gave Cleopatra such power? She wasn't the most beautiful woman the world has ever known, but she must have been fascinating. Poets and historians, both Greek and Roman, described her as a goddess. Her fame continues. Countless plays, operas, and movies have been produced about her. William Shakespeare's play *Antony and Cleopatra* is still performed today all over the world. Cleopatra's dramatic death has been the subject of dozens of paintings. Yet no one knows what she really felt about her Roman lovers. Did she truly care about Caesar or was he just a tool of her ambition? Did she fall in love with the handsome Mark Antony or did she use him in a desperate attempt to save the throne of Egypt?

These mysteries surround the Cleopatra of history. We may never know the answers.

CHAPTER 13

THE EMPEROR'S NEW NAMES

THE REIGN OF AUGUSTUS

AUGUSTUS AND SUETONIUS

"When I was 18 years old . . . I raised an army and used it to bring freedom back to the Roman state. I spent my own money to do it. . . . Because of this, the Senate passed a special resolution to make me a senator." These words were written by Julius Caesar's great-nephew: the first person to serve as a Roman general and member of the Senate while he was still a teenager.

Augustus, *My Achievements*, 14 CE

Julius Caesar, who had no **legitimate** sons of his own, was especially fond of his sister's grandson, Gaius Octavius. When his sister Julia died, the dictator chose 12-year-old Octavius to deliver his grandmother's funeral oration. Five years later, in 46 BCE, Octavius rode with his great-uncle in his triumphal procession into Rome. The next year, the young man joined Caesar's military campaign in Spain. The dictator believed that someday his great-nephew would do great things for Rome.

"Legitimate" comes from the word *legitimus*, which is kin to the Latin word for law, *lex*. A "legitimate" child is one whose parents are married to each other.

After his victories in Spain, Caesar planned a war against the rebellious tribes of Illyria, a region across the Adriatic Sea. Putting young Octavius in charge, he

In this first-century statue, Octavius wears a fancy breastplate showing the heroes of Roman mythology. The actual suit of armor was discovered in his wife's villa near Rome. The small statue of Cupid shows Octavius's divine ancestry as a descendant of Venus, the mother of Cupid.

WHAT'S IN A NAME?

The Romans called Gaius Julius Caesar Octavianus by the name "Caesar," but we have three other names for him as well. We call him Octavius (his given name) when he was young, Octavian after Julius Caesar adopted him, and finally Augustus after he is given this honorary title.

sent the army to Illyria with instructions to wait for him there. Then Caesar returned to Rome to begin reforming the government—a big job. Caesar set to work with energy and determination. But his plans were foiled by the daggers of his enemies, when he was assassinated on the Ides of March.

Eighteen-year-old Octavius was in Illyria when he got news of his uncle's death. He made up his mind to return to Rome. While he was packing to leave, a second messenger came with the surprising news that, in his will, Caesar had adopted Octavius as his son and made him the heir to an enormous fortune. This news was sure to raise eyebrows—and perhaps some swords—in Rome.

Although he was still an inexperienced teenager, Octavius was suddenly a public figure. He would soon be plunged into the cutthroat world of Roman politics. His mother and stepfather saw how dangerous this could be. They tried to persuade him to stay away from Rome. But Octavius was determined, and he set out to claim his inheritance. As a first step, he took his adoptive father's name and combined it with his own birth name. He became Gaius Julius Caesar Octavianus.

Rome, meanwhile, was in the hands of Caesar's deputy, Mark Antony. He had seen the assassination and moved quickly to grab power. Octavian was not yet in Rome, so Antony delivered Caesar's funeral oration. His speech helped to persuade people that the dictator's assassins were the enemies of Rome. With lightning speed, Antony took over Caesar's money, property, and all of his official papers.

This was not what Caesar had wanted. In his will, he promised a generous gift of money to every Roman citizen. But Antony refused to honor the murdered hero's wish.

When Octavian reached Rome, he honored his great-uncle by giving his own money to the citizens. With the help of Cicero's speeches and with Caesar's veterans marching behind him, Octavian earned the support of the Senate. Not only was he elected to the Senate, he also became a consul—even though, according to Roman law, he was too young to hold these offices. Octavian bragged about it when he later wrote his memoirs.

For about a year, Octavian and Antony battled for control, but they finally became allies. They joined with Caesar's general Lepidus to form a triple alliance, the Second Triumvirate. The three men, called *triumvirs,* were determined to hunt down Brutus and the other **conspirators** in Caesar's murder. Some suggested that Brutus be decapitated, and his head brought back to Rome and thrown at the feet of Julius Caesar's statue.

cum + *spirare* = "together" + "breathe" Conspirators "breathe together"—secretly plot in whispers, as did the murderers of Julius Caesar

Antony and Octavian left Lepidus in charge of the government while they went off with their armies to find the assassins of Julius Caesar. At Philippi in northern Greece, the *triumvirs* were victorious and Brutus committed suicide. Even though Antony was the more successful general and Octavian was sick during the decisive battle, all three men claimed victory and divided the empire among themselves.

Octavian and Antony may have been partners, but they were never friends for long. While Antony was busy reorganizing Roman territories in the East (and meeting Egypt's queen, Cleopatra), Octavian **confiscated** land in the Italian countryside and gave it to retired soldiers as a reward for their services. Because of these landgrabs, trouble flared again between the two leaders. Antony's wife and brother led a rebellion against Octavian while Antony was away.

"Confiscated" stems from the Latin word *fiscus,* which originally meant a woven basket or chest, but later came to mean "the imperial treasury." When something is confiscated, it is taken by the authorities.

Mother Earth basks among the symbols of plenty—birds, animals, fruit—that Italy enjoyed during Augustus's reign. This marble carving is from the Altar of Augustan Peace, which was built in 13 BCE *and dedicated in 9* BCE.

Octavian built the Altar of Peace shown on this coin. The letters S *and* C *stand for* "Senatus Consulto," *which tell us that it was produced "by the order of the Senate."*

When Antony heard about it, he had to come home to deal with the crisis.

By 30 BCE, the war had ended. Antony was dead, and Octavian had defeated all of his rivals. At 33 years of age, he was suddenly the master of the Roman world.

Octavian wanted everyone to know that he had brought peace to Rome after decades of civil war. He called it the *Pax Romana,* the Roman Peace, and built an elaborate Altar of Peace on the main road leading into Rome to celebrate his accomplishment. Octavian also demonstrated his victory by closing the doors of the temple of Janus—the god with two faces who guarded the doors of homes and cities. By tradition, these doors were kept open in times of war so that Janus would be free to help Rome against its enemies. In 500 years of almost-constant war, the temple doors had only been closed twice.

Rome was at peace, but its government was a mess. Enemies along the frontiers had taken advantage of Rome's turmoil by rebelling against its control or refusing to pay its taxes. Octavian had to overcome these troublesome neighbors, but he also had to quiet the quarrels among the leaders of Rome. It was tricky to keep the Senate on his side while attacking corruption within it.

Hundreds of senators had died in the civil wars. Octavian filled their places with men who had been loyal to him over the years. Many of these new Senate members were not from Rome, but from other Italian cities. Men like Octavian's best friend, his general Agrippa, formed the new ruling class. Octavian chose them not for their family ties, but for their ability and loyalty.

Although Octavian was wise enough to avoid the title of king, he accepted the name of Augustus in 27 BCE.

Augustus, *My Achievements,* 14 CE

> After I had put out the fires of civil war, . . . I transferred the Republic from my power to the control of the Senate and people of Rome. For this . . . I was named Augustus by the Senate. . . . From this time on, I topped everyone in influence.

Augustus Caesar, now the emperor of Rome, worked to reorganize the government and the military. His greatest accomplishment was the creation of a system of government that lasted in Rome for five centuries: the Roman Empire.

Augustus created Rome's first police and fire brigade. He created a network of roads that connected the major cities of the empire, linking them all to Rome. He changed the way finances were handled and issued new gold and silver coins. He gave free food to the poor. He built the Forum of Augustus and decorated it with statues of his ancestors. He beautified the city and boasted of this accomplishment: "I found a city made of brick and left it a city of marble." Augustus also sponsored artists and poets like Horace and Virgil, whose works glorified Rome—and, of course, himself.

“ Suetonius, *Life of Augustus*, 130 CE

Throughout his reign, Augustus never forgot that his great-uncle had been killed by jealous enemies who feared his power and popularity. Augustus pretended that his powers were all voluntarily given. He allowed freedom of speech and encouraged people to give him advice. But he was clever. He knew how to use power without seeming to seek or even treasure it. During his rule, magistrates were still elected to govern Rome. By sharing power with the magistrates, Augustus kept people from worrying that he was governing Rome alone. In fact, the soldiers were loyal to him and him alone—he paid their salaries and his treasury would pay their pensions.

The emperor's authority was so great that everyone left all the major decisions to him. But he was also very careful. Augustus kept a force of 4,500 soldiers to defend him. These soldiers, later called the Praetorian Guard, protected all of Italy. But some of them were always on hand to protect the emperor. To be on the safe side, the guards allowed only one senator at a time to approach the emperor, and they searched each man before he came close.

Augustus was a hard-working emperor. He traveled to many of the provinces under his care, but he was sickly and didn't expect to live very long. After his military campaign in Spain, Augustus returned to Rome and, in 23 BCE, became

OCTAVIAN'S CAREER

44 BCE
Murder of Julius Caesar; Octavius becomes Octavian

43-33 BCE
Second Triumvirate: Octavian, Antony, and Lepidus

42 BCE
Defeat of Brutus at Philippi

31 BCE
Defeat of Antony and Cleopatra at Actium

27 BCE
Octavian given name of "Augustus"

2 BCE
Augustus named "Father of the Country"

14 CE
Death of Augustus at age 77

quite ill and began thinking about a successor to follow him as Rome's ruler. His first choice had been his nephew Marcellus, but Marcellus had died young—not long after he had married Julia, the emperor's only daughter.

Julia played the key role in her father's search for a successor. After Marcellus died, she had to marry again, to a man of her father's choice. For her next husband, Augustus chose his general Agrippa, his closest friend and advisor. Although Julia was much younger than Agrippa, she dutifully married him, and the couple had five children. Then Agrippa died.

Although Augustus adopted his young grandsons as his heirs, he still needed a husband for Julia to protect the boys in the event of his own death. So he forced his stepson Tiberius to divorce his wife, even though Tiberius loved her very deeply. (He used to follow his former wife on the streets, weeping.) The marriage between Julia and Tiberius was a disaster: Julia was unfaithful, and Tiberius went into exile on the Greek island of Rhodes. Augustus was forced to banish his own daughter from Rome for her crime of adultery.

Julia must have spilled many tears over her father's marriage choices for her—especially the last one. She hated Tiberius, and he felt the same way about her. Even so, she would never have questioned her father's right to select her husbands. This was a parent's duty, especially if dad happened to rule the Roman Empire.

In spite of his poor health, Augustus lived to be 76 years old and reigned for 41 years as emperor. In the last years of his life, he realized that he must choose a successor. But whom? His beloved grandsons had both died young. With only one logical choice left, Augustus summoned his stepson Tiberius to Rome. He named this gloomy man as his coruler and successor.

In 14 CE, Augustus took a last journey by sea. He caught a chill in the night air and became quite ill. He called Tiberius to his bedside and spoke with him for a long time in private. Then, on August 19, knowing that the end was near, he called for a mirror and had his hair carefully combed. The biographer Suetonius tells the story:

"he summoned a group of friends and asked 'Have I played my part in the comedy of life believably enough?'" Then he added lines from a play:

> Suetonius, *Life of Augustus*, 130 CE

If I have pleased you, kindly show
Appreciation with a warm goodbye.

Augustus Caesar had played many roles well: the dutiful heir of Julius Caesar; the victor over Antony; the reformer of Roman government; the generous sponsor of literature and art; and, in his final years, the kindly father figure of Rome—providing food, entertainment, and security to his people. Near the end of his life, he remembered: "When I was 60 years old, the Senate, the equestrians, and the whole people of Rome gave me the title of Father of my Country and decreed that this should be inscribed in the porch of my house."

> Augustus, *My Achievements*, 14 CE

When Augustus died, all Italy mourned, and the Senate proclaimed him a god. His rule marked a turning point in history. In his lifetime, the Roman Republic came to an end. But he rescued the Roman state by turning it into a system ruled by emperors—a form of government that survived for another 500 years. In an age in which many rulers were called "saviors" and "gods," Augustus Caesar truly deserved to be called the savior of the Roman people.

SUETONIUS AND TACITUS

CHAPTER 14

MISERY, MISTRUST, MADNESS, AND MURDER

THE SUCCESSORS OF AUGUSTUS

Suetonius, *Life of Claudius*, 130 CE

My dear Livia,

As you suggested, I have discussed with Tiberius what we should do about your grandson Claudius. . . . The question is this: does Claudius have—shall I say—full command of his senses? . . . If he turns out to be physically or mentally handicapped, the public must not be given the chance to laugh at him . . . or at us.

The biographer Suetonius records this letter written by the emperor Augustus to his wife, Livia. Augustus was thinking ahead—far ahead. He had already named his stepson Tiberius as his **successor**, but he wanted to choose Tiberius's successor, too. By the end of Augustus's reign, the Roman Empire stretched from modern-day Portugal to Syria and from the English Channel to Egypt. Augustus desperately wanted to keep all of it in family hands.

"Successor" and "succeed" come from the Latin words *sub* (after or under) + *cedere* (to go). A successor follows, goes next. "Succeed" can mean "to follow" or "to do well."

Because all of his own grandsons had died, Augustus turned to Livia's children and grandchildren from her first marriage in his search for successors. Livia's grandson Claudius was a possible choice, but the emperor was prejudiced toward him. Claudius had suffered from polio in his early years, and the disease left him with a limp, a stutter, and an obvious twitch.

In the top scene of this cameo, Tiberius steps from his chariot to greet Augustus and the goddess Roma (wearing a helmet). Below, Roman soldiers capture foreigners conquered in battle.

ROMAN EMPIRE AT THE DEATH OF AUGUSTUS, 14 CE

He often had terrible stomach pains, he sometimes laughed uncontrollably, and he got a runny nose when he was angry. His physical problems, combined with his tendency to daydream, convinced Augustus that Claudius would not make a good emperor. Augustus and Tiberius talked about it and agreed not to give the young man any official duties. They decided that he should never take part in public ceremonies—he might embarrass the family.

Augustus had resisted naming Tiberius as his successor, and Tiberius resented it. The two weren't particularly fond of each other. Augustus found his stepson a gloomy fellow—quiet and sullen. The emperor was also impatient with his stepson's odd ways. Perhaps it bothered him that Tiberius loved his pet snake so much that he took it with him everywhere, even when he traveled. According to Suetonius, Tiberius sometimes had acne, and he was left-handed, which some people thought were bad signs. But in many ways, he was a good choice.

Suetonius, *Life of Tiberius*, 130 CE

> Tiberius was strongly and heavily built, and of above average height. . . . His body was perfectly proportioned from top to toe. His left hand was . . . so strong that he could poke his finger through a newly-plucked apple or into the skull of a boy or young man.

When Augustus died in the year 14, Tiberius came grudgingly to the throne. Even with a permanent chip on his shoulder, he ruled well—at first. He believed in free speech, refusing to punish people who spoke against him. He was careful with public money and left the Roman treasury 20 times larger than when he came to power.

But as the years passed, Rome's second emperor became more and more suspicious of the people around him. He listened to the gossip of malicious men who filled his ears with stories of hidden enemies and secret plots. The emperor believed the lies he heard and ordered the executions of many innocent men. In the end, no one in Rome felt safe. A person could be suddenly arrested and killed—yet never know the reason why. Everyone wondered who would be next.

Like Augustus, Tiberius wanted to choose his own successor. After his nephew and son both died mysteriously—probably poisoned—Tiberius abandoned Rome. He moved to the island of Capri and left the government in the hands of his friend and advisor, Sejanus—the only man in the world whom Tiberius still trusted.

But Tiberius had chosen badly. Sejanus was a traitor. He worked against his emperor and later led bloody persecutions against the descendants of the great Augustus. When Tiberius discovered the truth about Sejanus, he was terrified. He feared that the Praetorian Guard, commanded by his former friend, might rise up against him. So he hinted—aloud—that he might adopt Sejanus as his successor. It was a trick, and it worked. Sejanus grew both proud and careless. Tiberius waited for the right moment, then secretly replaced Sejanus as commander of the Guard. He then ordered his former ally executed.

RIGHT IS RIGHT, LEFT IS SINISTER

In Rome, as in many ancient cultures, "left-handedness" was believed to be unlucky. The Latin word for the left hand is *sinister,* which in English means evil or unfortunate. The opposite of *sinister* is *dexter*—the right hand or right side. Birds flying in the right-hand side of the sky promised good luck . . . on the left, bad luck. Someone who is "dexterous" is skillful or agile.

Near the end of his life, Tiberius adopted his great-nephew Gaius as his successor. Gaius was eager to rule—so eager, it was whispered, that he murdered his uncle with a slow-acting poison. The murder charge was never proved, and in 37 CE Gaius became the third emperor of Rome.

As a boy, Gaius had lived among his father's troops in Germany and was always dressed as a miniature soldier. Papa dressed him in tiny military boots. This practice earned Gaius the nickname Caligula, which means "Little Booties."

Because he was the great-grandson of much-loved Augustus, Caligula was popular in the early months of his reign. For a while, he ruled well: he reduced taxes and put on many public entertainments for the people. But, in the words of his biographer, Suetonius, Caligula changed completely after those early years. "So much for Caligula the Emperor," writes Suetonius, "the rest of this history must deal with Caligula the Monster."

“ Suetonius, *Life of Caligula*, 130 CE

How did this popular young man become a crazed tyrant? This mystery has puzzled scholars for hundreds of years. The strongest theory is that he had a brain disease that drove him insane. Whatever the cause, there can be no doubt: Caligula was a madman. He murdered senators to steal their property or take their wives. He gave Rome's far-away provinces to his boyhood pals. He married three of his sisters and insisted that the people worship him as the god Jupiter. He was so fond of his horse, Incitatus, that he built him a marble stable with an ivory stall. He planned to make Incitatus a consul but was assassinated before he could make the appointment official. Imagine: a horse in the Senate!

Understandably, the Senate was relieved when Caligula was assassinated by officers in his own Praetorian Guard. After his terrible reign, many people argued that Rome should forget about emperors and go back to being a republic. But the military leaders disagreed. Their power was greater under the emperors, so they insisted

Caligula had just come to power when this bust was sculpted. Scholars can name 37 CE as its date because his image is almost identical to what appears on coins minted in that year.

on finding a successor to Caligula. The problem was who? There was almost no one left in the imperial family—except Caligula's bumbling old uncle, Claudius. But where was Claudius? No one knew.

"Palace" comes from the Latin word *palatium*, since the emperors lived in the imperial mansion on the Palatine Hill in Rome.

According to Suetonius, when news came that Caligula had been assassinated, Claudius was afraid that he would be killed, too. There was no time to escape, so he hid behind some curtains in the **palace**. An observant soldier spotted his feet beneath the drapes and dragged him out, thinking he was a prowler. By chance, someone recognized him and, within a day, Claudius was acclaimed the fourth emperor of Rome.

This was the limping, stuttering grandson about whom Augustus had written in his letter to Livia. Because of Claudius's disabilities, the imperial family had mostly ignored him. He wasn't very interested in politics, so he was allowed to go his own way—free to study history and write books. Although Tiberius and Caligula had murdered other members of the family, Claudius quietly survived. No one bothered to kill him. He was harmless and a bit feeble-minded. Wasn't he?

Actually, Claudius was very bright. As a young man, he studied with the great historian Livy and learned Etruscan, a complicated language that no one spoke by his time. Although he wrote his autobiography and a history of Rome in Latin, his 20-book history of the Etruscans was written in beautifully polished Greek—the language of high art. Unfortunately, all of these works are now lost.

This coin shows Nero looking pudgy, self-centered, and self-satisfied. He had already lost the image of the promising young emperor who would do great things for Rome.

Claudius ruled Rome very well for 13 years. He established a strong system of government and successfully invaded Britain. He gave citizenship to Roman subjects in faraway provinces and welcomed their representatives in the Senate. He passed laws requiring more lenient treatment of slaves. He was smart, except when it came to women—and there, he was very foolish. His fourth wife, Agrippina, poisoned him to make sure that her son Nero would inherit the throne.

Claudius's stepson, Nero, was 17 when he became the first teenaged emperor of Rome. The Romans welcomed his reign and believed that he would bring a new "golden age." For a while, it looked as if that might be true. During his first five years, Nero modeled himself on Augustus. He attacked corruption in government and returned power to the Senate. He made careful decisions in matters of law and government. It was a good start, but—like Tiberius and Caligula—Nero soon lost his way. Nero became more interested in performing on stage than ruling the Roman Empire. He loved singing more than anything else, and he craved applause. Nero sang at Greek festivals and won more than a thousand gold crowns for his performances. (In ancient times, performers or contest winners received crowns of victory, just as modern Olympic victors win gold medals.)

The spectacle of a singing emperor delighted the Greeks but disgusted the Romans. Nero's mother, Agrippina, agreed with the Romans. When she criticized her son's new passion for singing and performing, the emperor decided to murder her by sending her off in a boat that had a hole in it. The boat sank, but Agrippina swam ashore. Nero then hired a professional assassin to finish the job. Three years later, Nero also had his wife killed so that he could marry someone else.

Nero built an enormous new residence called the Golden Palace. Its entry hall featured a 120-foot-tall statue of the emperor himself, and its main corridor was a mile long. Nero spared himself nothing. He loved luxury, adored clothes, and refused to wear any outfit more than once. During his reign, no one else was allowed to wear purple—it was the imperial color. The emperor amused himself by playing the lyre, writing poetry, and racing chariots. Pleasure was his god. Cruelty was his style. One of his favorite "games" was disguising himself as a criminal, then going into the night to ransack shops and kill innocent people.

In July of 64 CE, a fire broke out and quickly spread across Rome. The damage was terrible, and the area around the imperial palace burned. Although Nero allowed his own gardens to be used as shelters and ordered a shipment of grain to feed the fire victims, he never received credit for these good deeds. The word in Rome was that Nero had

HUNGRY FOR APPLAUSE

The emperor Nero was so devoted to singing that he refused, for a time, to eat apples, because he believed they would damage his vocal cords. At times, he only ate chives marinated in oil, claiming that this was good for the voice.

started the fire himself. His enemies charged that he played the lyre and sang while the city burned. They claimed he did it so that he could rebuild his palace in grandeur without other, lesser buildings crowded around it. This tale is the source of an often-repeated phrase: "Nero fiddled while Rome burned."

Nero probably did not set the fire himself. But he did shamefully neglect the military. Finally the troops rebelled and chose a new emperor. When Nero heard that the armies had reached Rome, he committed suicide. As he thrust himself against a sword, he cried: "How great an artist dies in me."

“ Suetonius, *Life of Nero,* 130 CE

The four emperors who succeeded Augustus—Tiberius, Claudius, Caligula, and Nero—lived in his shadow. None ever felt secure on the throne. Their reigns were a pitiful parade of misery, mistrust, madness, and murder. In the end, the army turned away from the dynasty that had originally brought peace and prosperity to Rome. The horrible years after Augustus's death convinced many people that hereditary rule was a dangerous thing.

Civil war returned to Rome after Nero's suicide. One general after another marched on the capital city. In 69 CE, it seemed that anyone with an army could become the

Rome is burning in this 18th-century French painting. Many people thought that Nero started the fire so that he could build a new palace.

emperor of Rome. This savage year, called the Year of the Four Emperors, ended with the triumph of Vespasian.

Vespasian, a soldier from the Italian middle class, was completely different from the emperors who preceded him. The historian Suetonius applauds his goodness:

> My researches show that no innocent person was ever punished during Vespasian's reign except behind his back or while he was away from Rome. . . . He never rejoiced in anyone's death and was often known to weep when convicted criminals were executed.

Suetonius, *Life of Vespasian,* 130 CE

The new emperor was practical and thrifty. Because Nero's years of wild spending had left the empire bankrupt, Vespasian was forced to raise taxes. At one point, his son complained that the tax on Rome's public toilets was crude. The emperor held a coin under the young man's nose. "Does this money smell bad to you?" he asked.

Suetonius, *Life of Vespasian,* 130 CE

Vespasian's reforms restored the economy and kept the soldiers loyal. At last, the emperor no longer had to be tied to the leaders of the past—not to Julius Caesar, nor even to Augustus. The leadership of Rome had changed, and, with it, the future. Nero had built an enormous palace for himself in the center of Rome. On the same spot, Vespasian began building the Colosseum, a center for the people's entertainment. When his son, the Emperor Titus, launched the Colosseum's opening games in 80 CE, the people's wishes were first and foremost.

Sadly for Rome, Titus ruled only from 79 to 81 CE. He was succeeded by his brutal brother, Domitian, who ruled until 96. Once again, a tyrant sat on the imperial throne. Although Domitian was a successful general, his reign was marked by book burnings, plots, and executions. Domitian died the way he had lived: in a palace conspiracy. Even his wife took part in the plot against him. The historian Tacitus tells how hard it was to be in the presence of such a monster: "It was no small part of our sufferings that we saw Domitian and were seen by him. Our sighs were noticed by him, and his cruel eyes saw whenever we turned pale. His red face made sure that he never blushed from shame."

Tacitus, *Life of Agricola,* 98 CE

CHAPTER 15

“ PLINY THE YOUNGER, INSCRIPTION FROM GAUL, VALERIUS MAXIMUS, CATULLUS, INSCRIPTION FROM ROME, HORACE, SUETONIUS, AND JUVENAL

CHILDHOOD AND MARRIAGE, MOTHERS AND MATRIARCHS

WOMEN AND CHILDREN

Calpurnia was a teenager when she married 40-year-old Pliny. He had been married twice before and was already well known in Rome as an orator, politician, and writer. In a letter that he wrote to Calpurnia's aunt, Pliny praised his young wife as

“ Pliny the Younger, *Letters*, 105 CE

> sensible and very thrifty. She has even . . . taken an interest in literature. She has copies of my books. She reads them over and over again. . . . She sets my poems to music and sings them. . . . No musician has taught her, only love itself—the best teacher of all.

Blandinia Mariola, another young wife, married when she was 13 years old and died at 18. She and her husband, Pompeius, lived in the province of Gaul. Pompeius was not an aristocrat or a writer like Pliny. But because of his job, we know his thoughts and feelings. Pompeius worked as a plasterer, and when his wife died, he wrote her epitaph in plaster: “Pompeius Catussa . . . dedicates this memorial to his wife, who . . . lived with him for 5 years, 6 months, and 18 days. You who read this, go bathe in the public baths of Apollo, as I used to do with my wife. I wish I still could.” Although we don't know the cause of Blandinia's death, it's likely that she died in childbirth, as many women did in those times. Her husband clearly loved her and was overcome with grief when she died.

“ Inscription from Gaul, 2nd century CE

Blandinia and Calpurnia were both deeply loved. But a woman with a violent husband could be in danger. Roman law allowed a man to beat his wife if she was unfaithful or if she just made him angry. In the first century CE, Valerius Maximus, in his collection of anecdotes, writes about a man who "beat his wife to death with a club because she had drunk some wine." He was not punished or even criticized for killing her.

Valerius Maximus, *Memorable Deeds and Words*, 35 CE

When a girl married, she left her father's control only to come under the power of another man: her new husband and perhaps also her father-in-law, if he was still alive. She was usually between 14 and 17 at the time of the wedding. Her husband would likely be in his mid-20s. Aristocratic parents arranged marriages for their children, often when they were very young. The wishes of the parents were much more important than the wishes of the couple.

A pretty young girl ponders what to write in her book. She lived in Pompeii, a city later destroyed when a volcano erupted in 79 CE.

Weddings were simple. The bride and groom didn't need a marriage license. All they had to do was to declare in front of witnesses that they wanted to be married, and the marriage was official.

In ancient Rome, a woman's greatest purpose was to have children. But sometimes, if poor parents couldn't afford to take care of their children, they might leave a newborn baby outside to die. Daughters were less valued than sons, so infant girls suffered this fate more often than boys. Even the naming of girls could be impersonal. Daughters were given a version of their father's name and simply numbered. For example, a man named Clodius might call his three daughters Clodia Prima, Clodia Secunda, and Clodia Tertia—Clodia One, Two, and Three. An unmarried daughter was considered a burden because she couldn't produce sons to carry on the family name. The Roman poet Catullus gives this advice to an unmarried girl: "Do not refuse . . . a husband, little girl. It's not right to reject the man to whom your father and mother gave you. You must obey them."

Catullus, *Poems*, 54 BCE

But Roman law didn't completely neglect women. They had some protection. By law, they had the right to own property. If a girl's father died without making a will, she received a portion of his wealth, just as her brothers did. Wealthy

Roman women built temples, paid for public games, and donated to the treasuries in their home cities. They had much more social freedom than women in many other ancient societies. They went to public events and banquets and were not separated from men as much as Greek women were.

Roman childhood was short. For aristocratic girls, childhood ended early because the girls married young. Poor children, both boys and girls, had almost no time for play or school—they had to work. Rural children began to work in the fields when they were very young. City children had jobs such as shop assistants, messengers, cleaners, and apprentices. Archaeologists have found epitaphs for two nine-year-old girls. Both had jobs when they died. One was a hairdresser, whose mother, Hilara, put up her tombstone. The other was a gold worker, probably an assistant to a jewelry maker: "In memory of Viccentia, a very sweet girl, a worker in gold. She lived nine years."

“ Inscription from Rome

Aristocratic children were luckier than poor ones. They had some of the same toys that modern children enjoy: dolls and model soldiers. They used walnuts as "marbles" and played with balls, hoops, and sticks. Wealthy children could go to school, and **education** was important to their families. Learning began at home with the mothers in charge, but later fathers took over. Very wealthy parents hired private tutors, but most children went to elementary schools where they studied reading, writing, and math. They learned through chanting and memorizing because books were rare and expensive. They had chairs but no desks. They wrote on wax tablets that could be "**erased**" and used again. Since school usually started before dawn, each student brought a lamp to school. These lamps burned animal fat—usually from pigs—which was smelly and smoky. Archaeological digs have uncovered books and school materials covered in sticky, black soot.

Educare = "to rear," "to train," "to draw out." At its best, education draws out a person's natural understanding and wisdom.

Eradere = "scrape" or "scratch out." Roman students often wrote on wax tablets, using a writing stick called a *stylus*. If they made a mistake, they erased it by scraping the wax clean.

Teachers had to provide classroom space for their students. But not all teachers could afford to rent or buy the rooms their students needed. So some of them taught outdoors, regardless of the weather. They gathered their students on the sidewalks or in the market square, competing with traffic noise and the sounds of a busy city at work.

When the poet Horace was a schoolboy, one of his teachers was Lucius Orbilius. Horace remembers him as a teacher "who loved the whip." Another writer, Suetonius, describes Orbilius's "fiery temper which he unleashed not only on his rival teachers, . . . but also on his students." Many, many Roman boys studied with Orbilius and felt the sting of his whip—he lived to be a hundred years old.

Horace, *Epistles,* 15 BCE

Suetonius, *A Book about Schoolteachers,* 120 CE

Poor boys followed their fathers into the fields or shops to learn their trade. But the sons of nobles went with their fathers and uncles to the Assembly, the law courts, and even the Senate. At 16, young noblemen sometimes went on military campaigns with their relatives, just as Octavius did when he went with Julius Caesar to fight in Spain. These boys learned the duties of Roman public life by watching and copying family grown-ups at work.

Schooling ended for girls, even wealthy ones, when they were around 11. They were expected to prepare for marriage at home. Even so, some Roman women managed to become very well educated. Juvenal, a satirist of the second century CE, found this annoying. "Still more exasperating is the woman who wants, as soon as she sits down to dinner, to talk about poets and poetry. . . . Wives shouldn't try to be public speakers . . . and they shouldn't read the classics. There ought to be some things women don't understand."

Juvenal, *Satires,* 120 CE

Rome's history, as it comes from the earliest sources, is mostly about men. It was written by men and for men. A woman had no identity of her own. Most women were thought of as somebody's mother, wife, or daughter. They were not allowed to serve as government officials, senators, or military commanders. But beginning with the rule of Augustus Caesar, aristocratic women began to have more influence. The wives and daughters of the emperors exercised real power, far more than ever before.

Sad parents buried these toys in their child's tomb. They believed that the child would want toys to play with in the afterlife.

Augustus's wife Livia was an extraordinary person. Her first husband, a much older man named Tiberius, had sided with Mark Antony against Octavian (who later became the emperor Augustus). When Antony's forces were defeated, Livia and Tiberius—with their infant son, also named Tiberius—escaped from Rome and became fugitives, hiding first in Sicily and then in Greece. When it was finally safe for them to return to Rome, Octavian met Livia for the first time. He was stunned by her beauty and intelligence. For him, it was love at first sight. And he made up his mind to marry her, even though she and her husband were expecting their second child. He divorced his own wife and forced Tiberius to divorce Livia.

"Matriarch" comes from *mater,* which means mother. Like *pater* (meaning father) and patriarch, it points to the person who leads a family and is its strength.

Augustus ruled an empire, but he was not physically strong. Livia was the **matriarch** who nursed and counseled him for the 52 years of their long marriage. They had no children together but were devoted to each other.

It was well known in Rome that Livia advised her husband on political matters. Some ancient writers described her as an evil power behind the throne. Perhaps they painted a dark picture of her because they disapproved of a woman having such an influence on the emperor. It's possible—but not certain—that Livia didn't stop at simply giving advice. She was determined for her son Tiberius to succeed Augustus. And it was whispered by some that she arranged for the murders of her son's rivals. Maybe she did; maybe she didn't. But Tiberius *did* become the second emperor of Rome.

This stove's charcoal burners could be taken from room to room to keep a family warm. Benjamin Franklin invented a very similar one, though he never saw this one from the first century CE.

Livia may have helped her son to the throne, but she and Tiberius didn't get along very well. Augustus had depended upon her during his years on the imperial throne. And when her son succeeded Augustus, Livia wasn't ready to give up her power. Time after time, she tried to control Tiberius, and it infuriated him. They even quarreled in public. Finally Tiberius left Rome and lived in Capri (an island off the coast of Naples), partly to get away from his mother. When Livia died in 29 CE, Tiberius didn't even go to the funeral.

Livia wielded her power behind closed doors, but in later years, women ruled more openly. The third-century

Slabs of meat hang from hooks in a butcher's shop. The butcher cuts a piece of meat with his cleaver while his wife figures the day's profits with her abacus.

emperor Septimius Severus was married to an intelligent woman named Julia Domna. When he was away from the city, fighting to maintain Rome's control over its huge empire, Julia Domna ran the government. She did the same thing when their son Caracalla was emperor (212 to 217 CE). A few years later, her niece Julia Mammaea went even further. When her son Alexander was emperor (from 222 to 235 CE), she ruled outright for a decade and even led Roman troops into battle. Though no Roman woman ever ruled in her own name, Julia Mammaea held the empire together during troubled times. And after she was murdered in 235, the empire tumbled into chaos for the next 50 years.

We have many Roman letters about women, but only a few by women have survived. With few written sources, archaeology has filled in the picture of daily life and how women and children lived in ancient Rome. Relief sculpture and funeral inscriptions tell us that women worked as nurses, waitresses, weavers, and food sellers. Urban women worked with their husbands as jewelry makers, leather workers, and ceramists.

But the very best images of ordinary people doing ordinary things come from the cities of Pompeii and Herculaneum. There, the lives of women, children, and men suddenly ended when a volcano erupted and killed every living thing for miles around.

CHAPTER 16

[66] **PLINY THE YOUNGER, PLINY THE ELDER, AND GRAFFITI FROM POMPEII**

A CITY TELLS ITS TALE

POMPEII AND THE ROMAN HOUSE

[66] Pliny the Younger, *Letters*, 105 CE

plumbum = "lead" (metal) For centuries, lead was the main metal used in plumbing. Scientists have now proved that lead poisons the blood and causes mental illness.

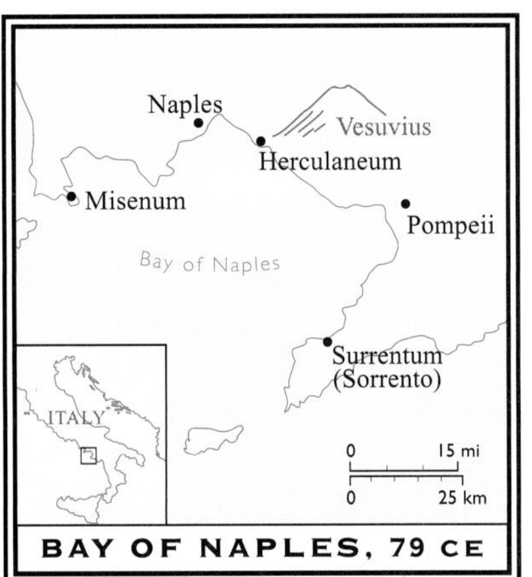

BAY OF NAPLES, 79 CE

The Roman writer Pliny the Younger describes the city of Pompeii as "one of the loveliest places on earth." People traveling in the first century CE to the city would have seen sheep grazing peacefully on the hillside. They would have noticed fruit trees and vineyards lining the road into town. As a prosperous market center, Pompeii had many visitors, especially traders. Sales of wool, cloth, and wine had made the city rich. It had a good supply of hotels, 20 taverns, and more than 100 bars where hot and cold wines were served until the wee hours of the morning. Pompeii also boasted temples, two theaters, a gymnasium, a gladiatorial school, an arena for games, public baths, and a public lavatory that flushed with fresh water. Nearly all Pompeian houses had indoor **plumbing**—water pipes and taps. Some families even had watering systems in their gardens.

Wealthy Pompeians ate very well. In fact, a dinner party in Pompeii was likely to be pretty fancy. The first course might be a platter of raw vegetables, olives, and sliced eggs. After this, perhaps some liver sausage would be served on top of polenta. The main course might be sweet and sour pork, rabbit served with a plum sauce, or stuffed kidneys—made with herbs, pine nuts, and fennel seed, and the fish sauce that the Romans used in almost everything. One possible dessert would be a pudding also made with fish sauce, followed by grapes, pears imported from Syria, and roasted chestnuts from Naples. Pliny the Younger and his uncle, Pliny the Elder, would have been used to fancy meals like these.

August 24, 79 CE had begun as peacefully as ever in Pompeii. There was no hint of the disaster to come. Pliny the Elder, a writer and Roman fleet commander, had spent a

Frightened people gather along the seashore hoping to escape the terrible fury of Mt. Vesuvius. English artist J. M. W. Turner painted the volcano in full eruption in 1817.

quiet morning at his sister's home in Misenum. He sat in the warm Italian sun for a while, then took a cold bath. Slaves brought his lunch, which he ate—as always—leaning against pillows, propped on one elbow. Then, well-fed and refreshed, he went back to his books. But at one o'clock, just across the Bay of Naples, the top of a mountain blew off with an ear-splitting crack, and an angry **volcano** tossed fire and molten rock into the air. Lava rolled down the sloping sides of Mt. Vesuvius, heading toward the helpless towns below.

"Volcano" comes from *Volcanus* or Vulcan, the Roman god of fire. A vulcanologist is an expert on volcanoes.

After the blast, people in Misenum saw a large, strange-looking cloud rising from the top of the mountain. Pliny the Younger later remembered that his uncle "climbed up to a place where he could get a better view. . . . It looked . . . like a pine tree, for it rose to a great height. . . . My uncle . . . was handed a message from Rectina [a family friend] . . . whose house was at the foot of the mountain. . . ." The terrified woman begged Pliny to rescue her and her family.

“ Pliny the Younger, *Letters*, 105 CE

Pliny the Elder boarded a ship and sailed toward Pompeii and Herculaneum, the very places from which everyone else was trying to escape. Although the danger was obvious, Pliny refused to turn back. A friend needed his help, so he went. He hoped that he could take Rectina and her household to safety aboard his ship.

When Pliny reached Rectina's house, he tried to reassure everyone, telling them that the danger would soon pass. But did he believe his own words? How could he? By this time, the afternoon sky was blacker than night. The house shook with every blast from the volcano. It swayed as the mountain spat fire and rock. The smells of soot and sulfur filled the air. People's eyes stung, and their throats burned.

Pliny the Elder was not only a loyal friend, he was also a very curious person. According to his nephew, he was "fearless and observed each new event and stage of the disaster, writing it all down exactly as he saw it. Ashes were already falling, hotter and thicker as the ships drew near, followed by bits of rock and blackened stones, charred and cracked by the flames."

" Pliny the Younger, *Letters*, 105 CE

In the midst of this terrifying crisis, everyone looked to fleet commander Pliny for advice. But Pliny wasn't sure what to say. He knew that, at any moment, Rectina's house could collapse and crush everyone inside. But it was dangerous outside too. Huge rocks, ash, and boiling mud spewed from the mountain's mouth and rained on the villages below. Pliny finally suggested that everyone should stay outside, tie pillows on their heads, and be brave. After taking a nap—and snoring loudly—he lit a torch and went down to the shore with a few slaves. But to his horror, he found the sea rolling wildly, boiling with melted rock. The last escape route was closed. It was too late. On the beach, Pliny began to stagger and gasp for breath as sulfur gasses filled his lungs. Unable to get enough oxygen, he collapsed and died.

DYING OF CURIOSITY

Pliny the Elder was one of history's most curious human beings. He was interested in *everything*. He wrote a 37-book encyclopedia in which he tried to describe and explain the entire world of nature, art, science—geography, medicine, plants, animals, minerals, farming, and ancient artists. In the preface, he wrote, "*Vita vigilia est.*" This means: "Life is being aware . . . alert."

At about the same time in nearby Pompeii, poisonous fumes had killed the owners of one house as they tried to hide their treasures in a well. They tumbled into the well along with their possessions. In another part of town, the priests of Isis were having a meal of eggs and fish when the disaster struck. Their bodies were later found with the sacred statues they tried to rescue. Modestus, a baker, died

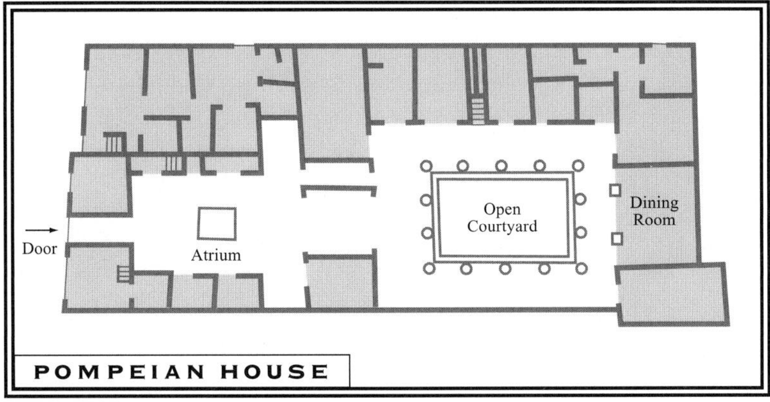

Many small rooms surround a central courtyard in this Pompeian house plan. These homes were built for privacy and light, and the floors were often decorated with colorful mosaics.

just after putting 81 loaves of bread into his ovens. Families who had just sat down to eat were killed in their homes and in the many restaurants of Pompeii. No one knows exactly how many people died. The lava killed some; others died from fumes, rocks, and suffocating ash.

Back in Misenum, Pliny the Younger, who was 18 years old, could hear the cries of terrified people as they poured into the streets and headed out of town. In a letter that he later wrote to his friend Tacitus, Pliny said that he and his mother stayed at home as long as they could, hoping for news of his uncle's safety. He tried to stay calm by reading a book, but finally "it seemed best to leave town because the buildings were shaking all around us."

“ Pliny the Younger, *Letters*, 105 CE

Mother and son joined the other villagers on the road. Many people begged the gods to protect them as more and more ash and rock fell around them. In his letter, Pliny the Younger described the deep darkness of that day. "Night hung over us, not like one that is overcast, without a moon, but like a room, where all the lights have been put out." He confessed that he thought the end of the world had come, that "all the world had perished with me." But at last the darkness lifted, and the sun shone through with a strange yellowish light. "Our trembling eyes saw everything changed, buried deep in ashes like snowdrifts."

“ Pliny the Younger, *Letters*, 105 CE

Pompeians were used to the volcano's rumblings, so they probably weren't worried at first. But the smart ones soon realized that, this time, the mountain meant business!

This man fell to the floor of his home in Pompeii as volcanic fumes overcame and killed him. Had he believed that the danger would pass? Did he wait too long to escape?

And they ran. Scholars estimate that 80 to 90 percent of Pompeii's people escaped to safety. Within a few hours, Pompeii was hidden beneath nearly 20 feet of stones and ash.

Pliny the Elder's body was found two days later. The lava had not buried his body, and his notes were safely tucked beneath him. He had been a scientist to the very end, writing down everything he saw until the very moment of his death. Pliny the Younger later wrote a description of all that happened on that fateful day. He based his report on his uncle's notes—a firsthand account of one of Nature's worst temper tantrums: the eruption of Mt. Vesuvius.

When 19th-century archaeologists first used modern techniques to explore the ancient remains of the city, they found hollow cavities—holes—in the volcanic remains. They soon realized that these holes were where the bodies of the dead had been. The lava and ash had turned rock hard, but the corpses had decayed and disintegrated, leaving a hard, empty shell. By injecting plaster into the spaces, investigators were able to recreate the person or animal that died there. The plaster casts showed children crouching in fear, dogs running, and a woman with her three servants, desperately trying to escape with jewels and silver in their hands. Slowly and carefully, archaeologists uncovered a city caught in the moment of its death. They found 18 people huddled in a cellar and, at the city gate, a man with a new pair of shoes. Was he perhaps a beggar who thought this was his lucky day because someone running from the city had dropped a pair of shoes?

Archaeologists have found an amazing amount of graffiti painted and scratched on the walls of Pompeii. It's as if the walls themselves want to speak and to remind us of the real people who once lived there. Among the messages are advertisements for wine (two glasses for the price of one), an apartment to rent, a sad goodbye message to someone who died, and an announcement of the show times for the next gladiatorial games. A political notice says: "Elect Gaius Julius Polybius aedile. He supplies good bread." An anonymous lover scribbled a message to his girlfriend: "Hail to you, Victoria, and wherever you go, sneeze sweetly." ("Sneeze sweetly" was a Roman way of wishing good luck.) An unhappy customer wrote on the walls of an inn: "Innkeeper, you sell us water and drink the pure wine yourself."

Graffiti from Pompeii, 79 CE

Someone wrote these lines—as if he knew what was soon to happen: "Nothing lasts forever. After the sun shines brightly, it sinks into the ocean. The moon that was recently full, wanes. And a strong wind often becomes a gentle breeze."

The eruption of Mt. Vesuvius destroyed Pompeii, but, in a strange twist of fate, it also saved it. The city was captured. And life as ordinary people lived it in first century CE Pompeii was held in a moment of time.

This mosaic dog from ancient Pompeii pricks his ears and bares his sharp teeth. As he crouches to attack, the words at his feet growl a warning: Cave Canem *("Beware of the Dog")!*

CHAPTER 17

“ COLUMN NEAR PHILIPPI, JOSEPHUS, CASSIUS DIO, PLINY THE YOUNGER, AND MILITARY DIPLOMA FROM PHILIPPI

ALL THE EMPEROR'S MEN

TRAJAN AND THE ARMY

Tiberius Claudius Maximus began his military career as a lowly cavalryman. During a war between Rome and Dacia (the present-day country of Romania), his courage in battle drew the attention of his officers. Maximus later erected a 9-foot-tall marble column near Philippi in modern-day Greece, to make sure his achievements would be remembered. The inscription tells us that Maximus was "promoted to corporal by the divine Trajan." And in 106 CE, the emperor presented him with military honors "for his courage in the Dacian Wars . . . because he captured Decebalus [the Dacian king] and brought his head to Trajan."

“ Column found near Philippi, 115 CE

That severed head changed Maximus's life. Now he was no longer a common soldier. He was a leader. And he owed it to Trajan, a capable emperor who maintained a good relationship with the army—the large, well-organized, and professional fighting force that had made Rome supreme.

In Trajan's time, the Roman army was divided into thirty legions of 6,000 men each. The soldiers were called legionaries, and all of them were Roman citizens. A senator sent from Rome commanded each legion. The legions were divided into centuries (groups of about 100 men),

A statue of a legionary soldier from Rome stands ready for battle wearing sandals, protective leggings, a helmet, and armor over his chest.

each headed by an officer called a centurion, such as Tiberius Claudius Maximus.

Centurions were the backbone of the army. They enforced discipline and led their men into battle. Centurions were not aristocrats. Like Maximus, they joined the army as foot soldiers or cavalrymen. Although they experienced battle firsthand, they could only hope for promotion if their commanding officers recommended them. Showing great loyalty or courage when it really mattered was how they became officers.

For Maximus, becoming a centurion brought more than the honor of leadership. It also brought a big raise in pay. In the second century CE, a foot soldier earned 300 *denarii* a year—not much to live on. A centurion's pay was more than 16 times as much. The lowest-paid centurion made 5,000 *denarii*. And the highest-ranking centurion, the *primus pilus* (first lance) who marched at the front of the formation, earned 20,000 *denarii* a year.

DEAR DAD, SEND MONEY

A soldier's pay did not allow for luxuries. One new recruit wrote home, asking for the money to buy a white horse. He begged his mother to convince Dad to send him the cash. Life would be so much easier if only he had a horse!

ROMAN EMPIRE UNDER TRAJAN, 117 CE

The early years of the empire saw few wars. During these years the troops were kept busy training, serving as police, and protecting their camps. The army was highly organized and tightly governed. Even Rome's enemies admired its military discipline. The Jewish writer Josephus had fought against the Romans in 66 CE, and although the Romans had defeated his people, Josephus later praised his former enemies: "For the Romans, the wielding of arms does not begin with the outbreak of war. They don't sit idly by in peace time . . . waiting for trouble to strike. Quite the opposite."

“ Josephus, *The Jewish War,* 75 CE

A legionary dressed for battle carried a large shield, a sword and two spears. He was well trained in the tactics of attack as well as defense. One battle formation that the Romans invented was called the *testudo* ("turtle"). The historian Cassius Dio tells how it worked in battle:

“ Cassius Dio, *Roman History,* 225 CE

> Heavily armed soldiers carrying oblong or curved shields form the outside of a shell. . . . Facing outward, they enclose the rest of the soldiers. Others—those with flat shields—stand close together in the center and raise their shields over their own heads and the heads of the other soldiers. Nothing but shields can be seen, and all of the men are protected.

Each legion had its own permanent fort made of stone. When on the march, the soldiers built a rectangular camp at each stop. Until 200 BC, legionaries weren't allowed to marry. But many had unofficial wives and children who lived in makeshift towns near the military camps. These women and children were called camp followers. The towns they lived in later developed into such cities as Bonn in Germany and York in Britain.

In peacetime, construction was a big part of the soldiers' lives. They built frontier walls, roads, aqueducts, canals, bridges, arches, baths, and temples. The remains of their labors still dot the landscape in western Europe and North Africa. Among other things, the Romans built 10,000 miles of roads in Italy and the conquered provinces. These roads, made of rock and sand, were designed for marching soldiers, but they also served merchants and traders. Roman roads lie beneath many modern highways. You can tell if a road in Great Britain or Europe was built on top of an earlier Roman road because it will be arrow-straight. Rome's system of roads is part of its **legacy.**

legatum = "benefit"
A legacy is anything that is passed down from one person, civilization, or generation to another. Rome's many legacies include the system of checks and balances that keeps any one person or group from having too much power in the U.S. government.

When parading before visiting officials, Roman soldiers often wore fancy dress uniforms with masks and red plumes on their helmets. This display of power and elegance must have boosted their spirits in quieter times. They also entertained themselves with dice games, visits to bathhouses, and theatrical shows.

After 20 years' service in the military, a legionary was eligible for retirement. He would receive land or the cash equal to 14 years' pay. No longer a soldier, he was free to marry and settle down. Most of these men stayed in the provinces near their friends and old comrades.

The army was a big part of the economy of the Roman Empire. It kept money flowing in two directions. People in the provinces had to pay taxes to Rome, which took money out of the provinces. But soldiers posted to the provinces spent their salaries where they lived, which put money back into the local economies. A lot of money changed hands, and people profited on both sides. The provinces became more prosperous under the emperors. And the empire itself grew to its greatest size during Trajan's reign, from 98 to 117 CE.

Trajan was different from the emperors before him. For one thing, the emperor Nerva chose Trajan as his successor because of Trajan's abilities. Trajan was not kin to Nerva, nor was he a powerful senator. But Nerva chose him anyway.

Nerva was an elderly senator when he took the throne in 96, after the murder of the tyrant Domitian. Although he ruled for only two years, Nerva started a new tradition that gave Rome excellent government for more than 80 years. Instead of adopting a relative as his successor, the emperor picked the man whom he thought would do the best job. And he made a good choice: Trajan, the commander of Rome's forces in Germany.

Another difference between Trajan and his predecessors was that during his reign, Trajan never took away anyone's

ROMAN BATHS

Roman baths have been found all over the empire. Only the wealthiest Romans had their baths in their own homes. Everyone else used bathhouses provided by the town. These were not just places for washing. Like modern health clubs and spas, they were meeting places where people could exercise, play games, conduct business, and visit with their friends. They could even have their legs waxed.

property. And he didn't execute anyone. Even traitors were only exiled. His letters show common sense and human kindness. He was concerned about people in need and distributed money to feed poor children in the countryside. He wanted to be Rome's best leader, not its best master. He wanted to guide, not control. That's why he got along so well with the senators. He treated them as his equals. He wanted to work with, not against, them. When Pliny became consul, he honored his friend Trajan in these words: "You have willingly subjected yourself to the laws, which no one intended to apply to the emperor. But you didn't want more rights than we have—yet, that's the very reason why we want you to have even more." He was Rome's best emperor since Augustus and deserved his title: *Optimus Princeps,* which means "best leader."

" Pliny the Younger, *Panegyricus,* 100 CE

A third difference—and an important one—was that Trajan came from the provinces. All earlier emperors had been born in Italy. Most came from Rome itself. But Trajan grew up in Spain. His father was a military man who served for a while as the provincial governor of Syria. His early life in the provinces kept Trajan from being drawn into the plots and schemes that kept Rome in such constant commotion. He was concerned about the empire as a whole. And whenever Rome's frontiers were in danger, he attacked.

Under Trajan's leadership, Rome extended its rule across the Danube River into Dacia. The conquest of Dacia added rich gold and silver mines to Rome's treasury. In 106 the emperor celebrated this victory by sponsoring months of games in the Colosseum. Trajan also pushed the imperial frontier into Mesopotamia (present Iraq) and all the way to the Persian Gulf. No other Roman general had ever reached the gulf. According to legend, Trajan broke down and cried when he got there.

A vivid picture of Roman soldiers and military life still stands in Rome. It is Trajan's Column, erected by the emperor to celebrate his victories and those of the army. Rising 110 feet tall, the white column is decorated with 150 battle scenes containing a total of 2,600 carved figures, each about one-third life-size. The column shows us Trajan himself, addressing the soldiers and sacrificing to the gods.

In addition to uniformed, heavily armed Roman legionaries, Trajan's column also depicts troops called auxiliaries. Although these soldiers were not citizens of Rome, they made up about half of the Roman army. They were valued fighters who offered special skills that Rome needed. Archers from the Near East knew how to shoot with bows and arrows. Slingers from Majorca (near Spain) were experts with large, deadly slingshots. They could launch huge rocks against the enemy. Many cavalrymen were skilled horsemen from Gaul and North Africa. They were colorful and dramatic, dressed in full suits of armor. Their horses wore armor, too—their faces and bodies were covered by chain mail (flexible armor made of joined metal links).

A statue of Trajan once topped this 110-foot-high column (inset), but it was later replaced by a statue of the Christian St. Peter. The bottom row of figures shows the bearded spirit of the Danube River rising to watch the Romans build a pontoon bridge over his waters. About 2,600 figures cover Trajan's tall marble column.

An auxiliary soldier earned about two-thirds of a legionary's pay. But when he retired, he received a valuable bonus: he and his family became citizens of Rome. This was worth waiting and fighting for. At the end of his service, the soldier also received a bronze diploma. About a million of these bronze plaques were issued between the years 50 and 250. But only about 500 plaques have survived. Why so few? Partly because people were poor, and bronze was valuable. Sold and melted down, a bronze diploma could become a vase, a platter, or perhaps a shield that would be used to defend the glory of Rome.

One diploma that survives belonged to a corporal named Reburrus, son of Severus, from Spain. The inscription tells us about some of the advantages of citizenship: "The emperor Trajan, in his seventh year of power . . . has granted citizenship to [the soldiers] themselves, their children and descendents and the right of legal marriage with the wives they had when citizenship was granted them. . . ." Once a soldier had been granted citizenship, his children could also vote, join the army, and enjoy all the privileges of

“ Military diploma from Philippi 105 CE

This legionary soldier is dressed for a parade. His bronze helmet protects his head, face, and neck.

Roman citizenship. Soldiers' sons volunteered as legionaries and helped to bring Latin and Roman civilization to their homelands.

For centuries, the army protected Rome's frontiers while providing a system for talented men to rise step by step, generation by generation. It wasn't an enormous force: 350,000 men to protect an empire of 60 million people. Size did not make the Roman army effective—organization and discipline did. Because of its army, the Roman Empire lasted for 500 years after the death of Augustus.

CHAPTER 18

PLEASING THE ROWDY ROMANS

GLADIATORS AND CIRCUSES

“ MARTIAL, FRONTO, SIDONIUS APOLLINARIS, ROMAN RECORDS, GRAFFITI FROM POMPEII, AND SENECA THE YOUNGER

The bleachers in the Colosseum were full, but the audience was growing impatient. The games were late in starting. People shouted and stamped their feet. The animals roared from their cages beneath the floor of the arena. The smells of animal manure, sawdust, and human sweat mingled with the tantalizing odors of roasting sausage snacks as the audience waited in the hot Italian sun. At last the trapdoors opened, and wild animals burst into the huge arena. A gory show began.

Martial, a Spanish poet who lived in Rome, wrote an eyewitness account:

> The terrified trainers prodded the rhinoceros until its anger flared hot. . . . With its double horn, it threw a heavy bear into the air as easily as a bull might toss a straw dummy. Then the rhino effortlessly lifted up two steers, and a fierce buffalo and a bison surrendered to him.

“ Martial, *On the Games*, 80 CE

What looks like the floor level of the Roman Colosseum is actually its basement, where the gladiators and wild animals waited before they went out to fight in the arena.

ludi = "games"
"Ludicrous" comes from the Latin word, ludus, which means "game." Something that is ludicrous makes us laugh.

This was just one of many public shows that the Romans called ***ludi,*** or games. The games often involved animals. Sometimes animals were chained to one another—a bear, for example, chained to a bull—so that neither could escape a battle to the death.

Staged hunts were popular, too. In this brutal sport, animals imported from all parts of the empire were set loose in the arena. Slaves dressed as hunters chased and slaughtered elephants, bears, buffaloes, and even exotic creatures such as crocodiles, pythons, and ostriches. But the "hunters" wore no protective clothing, and many were wounded or killed.

The games were usually bloody, and always colorful, loud, and free. The people expected their government to entertain them—the more noisily and violently, the better. Politicians used the *ludi* to gain favor with the people and court their votes. Fronto, a writer and politician of the second century CE, warns that an emperor should take care "not to neglect actors and other performers of the stage, the racetrack, and the arena, since the Roman people are devoted to two things: food and free shows. Political success depends as much upon entertainment as on serious matters."

“ Fronto, *Elements of History,* 165 CE

Two gladiators fight in the arena against a lion and a wild boar. Because they fought wild beasts, these gladiators were called bestiarii.

Fronto knew what he was talking about. He had seen court life firsthand as tutor to a future emperor, Marcus Aurelius, who ruled Rome from 161 to 180 CE. He knew that an emperor could even take away the people's voting rights and still be popular. All he had to do was keep the racetracks busy and the Colosseum full of exciting events.

Rome's *ludi* started out as religious festivals, honoring certain gods who controlled the harvest, the weather, and the hunt. The *Ludi Cereales,* for example, honored Ceres (the goddess of grain) and were celebrated every year in April. The biggest festival of the year was the *Saturnalia* in honor of Saturn, the god of agriculture. During this week-long celebration in December, the Romans exchanged gifts and threw extravagant dinner parties. These parties were unusual because, at this time only, masters waited on their slaves.

Gradually, more and more festivals were added as thanksgivings to the gods for military victories and to celebrate patriotic events. On the festival of the Lupercalia on February 15, for example, runners raced around the Palatine Hill and whipped the spectators with thongs made of goatskins.

The Romans also loved plays. At first they presented them on temporary wooden stages. The earliest surviving comedies were written about 200 BCE by Plautus, who took Greek plays and made them even more uproarious to please the rowdy Romans. Drama was so much a part of life that the Romans often used theatrical decorations in their homes.

Of all the public entertainments, chariot racing was the oldest, dating back to the time of Romulus, Rome's legendary founder. From the beginning it was a great crowd-pleaser. Rome's chariot races were held in an enormous race course called the Circus Maximus. As Rome grew and became wealthier, the Circus Maximus was expanded until it held 250,000 people. No stadium in the modern world holds so many spectators.

Although one emperor staged a chariot race with camels, most races had chariots pulled by four horses. The

This ivory statuette shows a heavily armored gladiator, covered from head to toe. His opponent might have only a net and a dagger, but at least he could move.

Roman poet Sidonius Apollinaris, writing in the fifth century CE, described a race in which his friend Consentius was one of the drivers. The chariots were decorated in different colors—red, blue, white, and green—so that the spectators could keep track of their favorite teams.

Before the race began, the horses reared up, snorting and prancing with excitement. Their grooms tried to soothe them as they kicked against the wooden gates that held them back. When the trumpet sounded, the horses bolted onto the track. The drivers, standing in their chariots, leaned forward so that they could whip the backs and even the shoulders of their horses, urging them faster, faster around the track. The chariots raced down the straightaway, jockeying for place as they made the turns. One of the drivers pulled out of the race; another lost control of his horses. Towards the end, only two teams remained in the race: Consentius and the fourth driver. Sidonius describes the race much as a modern sports announcer would:

“ Sidonius Apollinaris, *Poems,* 469 CE

> Consentius drives straight and fast. . . . The fourth driver pursues Consentius recklessly, hoping to overtake him. He cuts in sharply across the track. His horses lose their balance and fall. Their legs become tangled in the spinning chariot wheels. . . . The driver is hurled headlong from the shattered chariot. And now the emperor presents the palm branch of victory to Consentius.

Many Romans were addicted to the races and made large bets on the outcome. Competing teams of brightly decorated horses drew fierce loyalty from the spectators. People shouted for their favorites as the chariots crowded together on the turns, lap after lap. Fights and riots occasionally broke out among the fans.

A chariot driver put his life on the line each time he raced. He did it for the same reason that people do dangerous things today: for money, fame, and excitement. Some drivers became so wealthy that even emperors sometimes envied their riches. The Romans kept careful records. We learn from them that Diocles from Spain was very successful as a chariot driver. He raced for 24 years and won 1,462 races out of 4,257. He "was in the money 2900 times. He was second 861 times, third 576 times. . . . He failed to place 1351 times. . . . He won a grand total of 35,863,120 sesterces." How much money is that? Diocles's total winnings equaled a year's pay for 30,000 Roman soldiers.

“ Roman records, about 130 CE

Other public entertainments also drew the public's attention: footraces in a stadium and even mock sea battles staged in an artificial sea fought with full-sized ships. Though these battles were a pretense, the ships were real. So were the deaths of the men who died in the fighting.

The best-known of all the Roman games were the gladiatorial matches. **Gladiators**, like Spartacus, were chosen from the strongest, fiercest slaves. They were trained to fight in special schools where they learned to use various kinds of weapons and equipment. Often the battle raged between brute strength on one hand and agility and quickness on the other. One gladiator would wear protective armor, carry a curved shield, and be heavily armed. His opponent would wear almost nothing and be armed only with a net, a small dagger, and a trident—a spear with three prongs.

"Gladiator" comes from the Latin word *gladius*, which means sword.

Rome's largest gladiatorial shows were held in an **arena** called the Colosseum. Not all gladiatorial battles ended with a death. Sometimes a wounded gladiator would appeal to the crowd for mercy. If he had fought well or was popular, the crowd might beg the emperor to spare his life. If they thought he deserved to die, they would gesture with their thumbs, although historians are not sure whether the gesture was "thumbs up" or "thumbs down." The *ludi* gave the emperor a chance to show the people that he was on their side by sponsoring the games and by following their wishes when he spared their favorite gladiators. Most gladiators lived to fight many, many times. To their owners and trainers, they were valuable properties, almost like modern rock stars. And like rock stars, they had many devoted fans. Archaeologists have found ancient *graffiti* to prove it.

arena = "sand" or "dust"; "a sandy place"
Rome's Colosseum is an oval arena with a dusty sand floor, surrounded by rising rows of seats, like a modern football stadium. It has long been believed that when the gladiators entered the arena, they shouted to the emperor, "We who are about to die, salute you." It makes for good drama. Too bad it isn't true.

“ Graffiti from Pompeii, 79 CE

Written on the walls of Pompeii were these breathless words: “The slasher Celadus makes all the girls sigh,” and “The net fighter Crescens has captured the hearts of all the girls.”

Roman culture was full of violence, but most Romans weren’t bothered by its presence in their lives. Seneca the

HISTORIAN AT WORK:
AN INTERVIEW WITH PROFESSOR KATHLEEN COLEMAN

Kathleen Coleman, *professor of Latin at Harvard University, teaches a course called “Roman Games.” She has been a consultant to Hollywood and has participated in several television shows on the History Channel, the Discovery Channel, PBS, and the British Broadcasting Corporation (BBC).*

How did you become interested in the gladiatorial games?

I was translating the set of poems that Martial wrote about the games that the emperor Titus put on to celebrate the grand opening of the Colosseum in 80 CE. Martial wrote the poems to honor and flatter Titus. But they contain the most fascinating details. Martial describes beast hunts, mock sea battles, and gladiatorial combat, but also public executions. In one of these executions, a prisoner was dressed to look like Orpheus, a character in Greek mythology. The audience would have known the story very well. Orpheus was such a fine musician that he could charm even wild animals with the music of his lyre.

As the show began, the doomed prisoner stood in the arena, plucking the strings of his instrument while tamed animals walked calmly around him. But then a ravenous bear was released into the arena. The prisoner was defenseless, and the bear mauled and killed him. The audience found the surprise ending hilarious.

Were all the games this violent?

Definitely not. The Romans thought that criminals and prisoners of war deserved to die, however cruelly. In their eyes, these lives had no value. But gladiators represented a big investment. Just as some slaves were trained to read aloud to their masters, to teach children, or to do accounting, gladiators were trained to fight in the games, and each one fought in a particular style—net fighting, for instance. They were more like modern prize-fighters who only fight once or twice a year. And in between fights, they ate well, had good medical care, and received reasonable treatment.

Younger, a philosopher of the first century CE, was an exception: he found the gladiatorial games revolting. He writes: "There is nothing more harmful to one's character than going to these shows. . . . When I come home from one, I find that I am greedier and more aggressive. . . . I am more cruel."

Seneca the Younger, *Letters*, 60 CE

Many people believe that the gladiators had a 50-50 chance of survival—that one of them had to die. But that wasn't the case.

How do we know?
The gladiators' tombstones give us some of our best information—and they are found all over the Roman Empire. This tells us that the games were not just held in Rome itself but also in Syria, Turkey, France, and elsewhere. Gladiators, or their loved ones, boasted on the tombstones about their skills: how many times they went into the arena, how often they fought to a draw, and how many times they won. Even if a gladiator was defeated, his life might still be spared. One gladiator's tombstone shows that he lived to be 45, which was old in ancient times. He may have been a successful gladiator who retired and then taught in the gladiatorial schools.

Did any gladiators themselves write about their lives?
Nothing has been found, but mosaics provide another source of information for us. Mosaics are pictures made from small colored tiles that decorated people's floors and walls. They often show gladiatorial combat. In mosaics, we can see the weapons and armor of the gladiators. Sometimes the men are shown fighting, and sometimes we see them at the end of the match, with one left standing and the other lying defeated on the ground. Some mosaics show referees ensuring a fair fight.

Could women become gladiators?
They could, but it didn't happen very often. Women gladiators were a great novelty. People then, like people today, got tired of seeing the same things over and over. So a female gladiator was something new and different. Like the men, they had "stage names." The only two women gladiators that we know about were called Amazon and Achillia.

If you could go back in time and interview a gladiator, what would you ask him?
I'd have many questions, but one would be about living conditions. We know that some of the gladiators in Rome lived in barracks near the Colosseum. The rooms were about 11 feet square, but we don't know how many men lived in each room. I'd also want to know how it felt to live with other gladiators—eating, exercising, and practicing together—and then to go into the arena to fight "for real." These men usually fought in pairs, so they would have known each other quite well. Wouldn't it have been terrible to face a friend in a battle that could end in the death of one or both?

CHAPTER 19

HOW TO GET RICH IN ROME

BUSINESS AND TRADE

WOOL-MAKERS' BUILDING, STATUE FROM POMPEII, AND AELIUS ARISTIDES

In the forum—the main public square—of Pompeii stands a large, beautiful building with a puzzling inscription written over the door. It reads: "Eumachia, daughter of Lucius and a public priestess, built this building in her own name and that of her son, N. Numistrius Fronto—with its hall, covered walkway, and porches. She . . . used her own money."

Wool-makers' building, 50 CE

The inscription tells us who built the building, but not why. Archaeologists later discovered in Pompeii a statue of a woman who was also identified as Eumachia (yu-MAH-kee-ah).

It's almost certainly the same woman. The second inscription says: "The wool-makers dedicate this statue to the . . . priestess Eumachia, daughter of Lucius."

Wool-makers' building, 50 CE

Statue from Pompeii, 50 CE

By comparing the two inscriptions, scholars were able to figure out Eumachia's story. She must have come from a wealthy family because she used her own money for the building. Her husband was Numistrius Fronto, a prominent citizen of Pompeii whose name appears in other records found in the city's ruins. After his death, Eumachia became the **patron** of the wool-makers' association and built an elaborate building for them. In the dedication of her building, she includes her son's name in order to boost his political career.

"Patron" comes from the Latin word *patronus*, and is related to *pater* (father). A patron is a sponsor or protector.

The wool makers who used the building were not the people who sheared the sheep or handled the wool on its way to market. Slaves did that work. The wool makers owned the sheep and the shops where the cleaning, spinning, dyeing, and stretching of the wool was done. The members of the association showed their gratitude to Eumachia by placing a marble statue of her in the courtyard of the building that she had built for their use.

The countryside around Pompeii was full of sheep, and wool was big business. Eumachia's building was probably the main center in the region for the buying and selling of wool, yarn, and cloth. The wool makers also made deals with shippers who would export the wool to distant ports.

There were many wealthy men and women like Eumachia who lived in the cities but made their money from the produce of their land—from the sale of grain, olive oil, animal skins, and wool. The safest investment was land, but the really big profits came from trade.

Merchants sometimes transported goods over land, using carts and wagons pulled by animals. Transport by sea was cheaper, but it was very risky. A sudden storm could crash a ship against rocks or capsize it at sea. This could

The worker on the left combs a piece of newly woven and dyed cloth with a brush made of thistles and thorns. The person on the right carries a large rack for drying the cloth.

THE WELL-TRAVELED COINS OF ROME

How did Romans pay taxes, buy lunch, pay for a haircut, or purchase a room at a roadside inn? With Roman coins. Around 300 BCE, Roman mints began mass-producing coins in gold, silver, and bronze. These mints issued billions of coins during the years of the Roman Empire. Thousands of them have since been found in Italy as well as in what is now Germany, England, Israel, Tunisia, Turkey, and India.

During the years of the Republic, coins celebrated the characters of Roman myth and history. The earliest ones had pictures of gods and goddesses stamped on them. Later, generals such as Sulla and Pompey appeared on coins, but only after their deaths. No living Roman was pictured on a coin until Julius Caesar imitated the Greek kings and had his own face stamped on the coins of Rome. After Caesar, Augustus and his successors all glorified themselves this way.

mean the death of sailors and maybe the financial ruin of the ship's owner. Many Roman ships *did* go down, and their remains are still being discovered today.

In 1999, construction workers building an office at the train station in Pisa, Italy, uncovered nine well-preserved Roman ships. As soon as they realized what they had found, they stopped their work and immediately summoned archaeologists to the site. The first ship investigated was an imperial warship from the second century CE. It was nearly in one piece, with its wooden planks and frame still held together by copper nails. The second was even older—from the first century BCE—and it was still loaded with cargo. Italian archaeologists, led by project director Stefano Bruni, found the remains of cherries, plums, and olives, as well as containers of 2,000-year-old wine. (No one was brave enough—or foolish enough—to taste it!)

The cargo ship's hold also contained a lot of sand and stone, used to prop up the cargo and keep the ship evenly weighted in the water. When investigators analyzed the stones, they discovered that many of them came from the lava of Mt. Vesuvius. This means that the cargo probably began its journey somewhere near the Bay of Naples, not far from Pompeii and Mt. Vesuvius. Near another ship, archaeologists found a coil of rope, a wicker basket, and a leather sandal that someone had lost long, long ago.

No one knows whether these ships sank or were abandoned. But why would ships be found inland—near the Pisa train station, so far from shore? The answer lies in the path of the Arno River, which runs through the city. Over many centuries, sand and silt washing down the river filled the harbor and finally hid it completely. Many ancient writers had mentioned this harbor, but for many centuries, no one could say where it was. Its discovery is important not only to historians, but also to archaeologists, geographers, and geologists.

Archaeologists have also found Roman ships far from Italy. In Britain, for example, an 1,800-year-old troopship was discovered in 2001. It was buried in the mud of the Tyne River in northeastern England, near the border with what is now Scotland. Investigators found part of a Roman

Busy cupids are making, pouring, and tasting wine for the god of love in the House of the Vetteii in Pompeii.

cavalryman's helmet, part of an infantryman's shield, three bronze bowls, a fragment of a Roman cooking pot, and 64 coins. These clues suggest that the ship was bringing fresh troops to fight against northern invaders when it was wrecked in a storm. According to Paul T. Bidwell, who led the investigating team of archaeologists, "Potentially, this is a stunning find, as it would be the first Roman troop ship to be found anywhere in the world."

By studying where ships and other Roman artifacts are found, historians can track the paths of ancient ships, armies, and traders. The finds can be as large as a ship or as small as a coin. In 1999, Turkish archaeologists uncovered the remains of a Roman aqueduct in a thick forest. This huge water system was built between 355 and 440 CE and would have required thousands of workers. The imperial government would have paid them all with Roman coins.

Historians studying ancient texts and archaeologists studying ancient artifacts have built up a picture of Roman trade. Although few Italians took part in foreign trade, traders from all over the world used Rome as their marketplace. Goods of all kinds passed through the Roman Empire for export. In a villa near Pompeii, for example, archaeologists have found 100,000 jugs of wine ready to be shipped throughout Italy and beyond. The **import** trade was lively as well. German peddlers brought amber from the area around the Baltic Sea to Rome for jewelry making. One scholar estimates that 45 million quarts of Spanish olive oil reached Rome every year from 15 BCE to 255 CE. Merchants shipped food and rare raw materials, like colored marble, throughout the Mediterranean, along with paper from Egypt, purple dye from Syria, glass from Palestine, and ironwork from Spain. Asian caravans brought incense, ivory, pepper, and silk from Arabia, Africa, India, and China.

"Import" comes from the Latin word *portare,* which means to carry. So imports are goods carried in; exports are carried out.

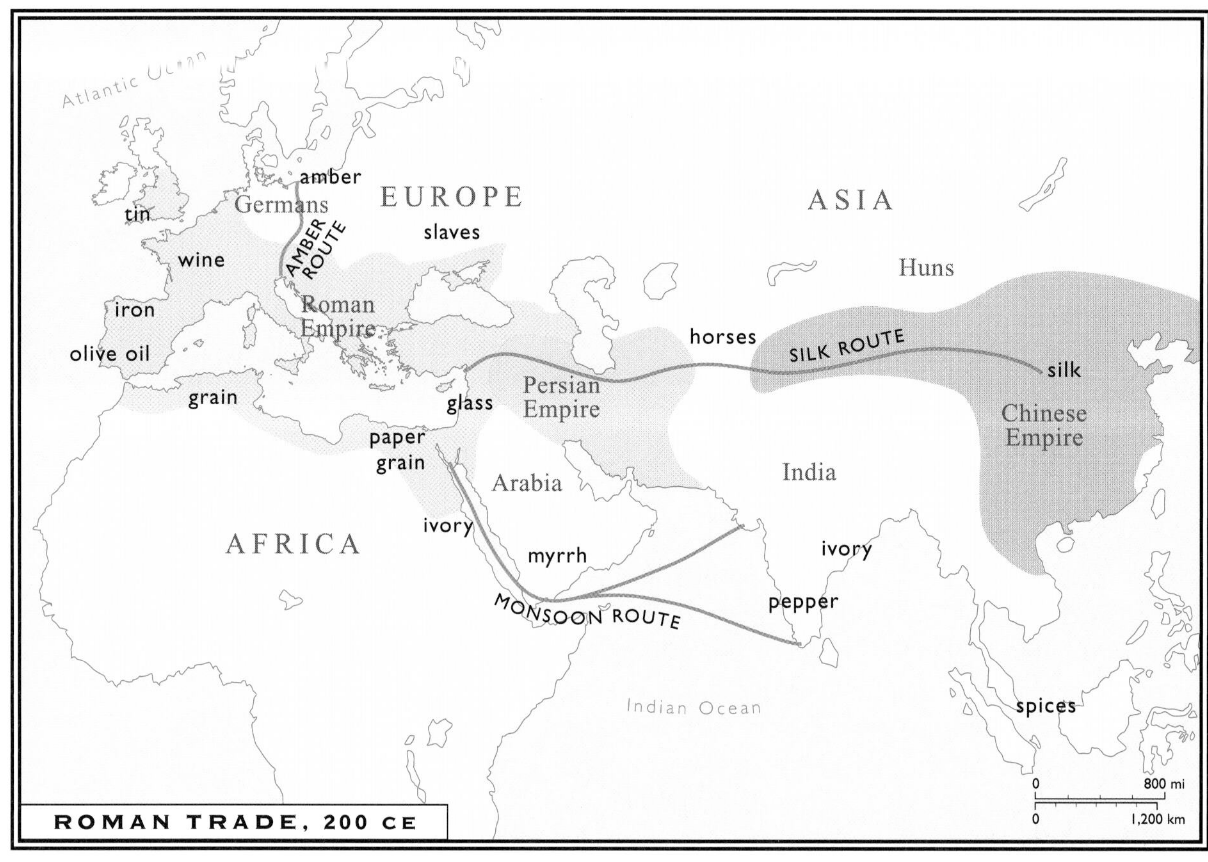

ROMAN TRADE, 200 CE

In the first century CE, Egyptian sailors discovered the secret of the monsoon—a strong wind in the Indian Ocean that changes its direction according to the season. In summer, the wind carried the Egyptian trading ships to India, and in winter it carried them back again. Soon after, Rome began to trade with India by sea and also opened a land route across Asia to China. Some Romans, including the scientist Pliny the Elder, hated to see so much Roman silver traded for foreign goods. But others thought Rome's busy, far-flung trade was exciting and wonderful. Aelius Aristides, a Greek of the second century CE, sums it all up in his praise of Rome: "Everything is shipped to Rome, from every land and every sea—the products of every season, of each country. . . . If anyone wants to see all these things, he must either travel through the whole world . . . or live in this city."

“ Aelius Aristides, *In Praise of Rome,* 155 CE

CHAPTER 20

THE RESTLESS BUILDER
THE EMPEROR HADRIAN

THE AUGUSTAN HISTORY, INSCRIPTION FROM AFRICA, AND PAPYRUS FROM BRITAIN

Hadrian's world changed completely when he was ten years old. His father died, and a distant relative adopted him. Suddenly Hadrian was no longer an ordinary boy growing up in Spain. Now guards and advisors from Rome protected him. And he had the very best tutors. Why? Because his distant relative just happened to be the Roman emperor Trajan. With no sons of his own, Trajan chose Hadrian as his heir.

Young Hadrian liked to study. Greek literature, art, and music especially fascinated him. His biographer writes that he "threw himself . . . into the study of Greek—so much so that some people used to call him the 'Little Greek.'"

Anonymous, *Augustan History,* 390 CE

Even after he became emperor in 117 CE, Hadrian found reading and writing poetry more exciting than running the government. He was a painter and a sculptor who worshiped beauty, both in art and nature. The practical Romans found this very strange. The senators didn't understand or trust this man who seemed to love Greece more than Rome.

Throughout his life, Hadrian grabbed every opportunity to travel to Greek-speaking lands. He was especially fond of Athens, where he completed an enormous temple of Zeus and built the graceful Arch of Hadrian that still stands today in the center of the city. The Athenians returned his devotion: they even elected him to local office.

The emperor Hadrian wears a full mustache and beard in this 2nd-century bronze statue. Hadrian was the first emperor to grow a beard. He did it to copy the Greeks, and then aristocratic Romans copied him.

Nearly all emperors traveled to the provinces to lead their armies or to attend to other official business. But Hadrian traveled because he was curious. He longed to experience the world, to see the great monuments of the Empire—such sights as the pyramids of Egypt, the Parthenon in Athens, and Sicily's great volcano, Mt. Etna. Once he "sailed to Sicily, and there he climbed Mount Etna to see the sunrise, which is many-hued, they say, like the rainbow."

Anonymous, *Augustan History*, 390 CE

Hadrian also traveled to make sure that the army, even in peacetime, was ready for battle. He took two long tours of the provinces; each one lasted for four years. Even though Hadrian had slaves to attend his every need, these journeys must have been strenuous. The emperor's friend Florus wrote a poem, making fun of Hadrian's long travels:

Anonymous, *Augustan History*, 390 CE

> I don't want to be emperor, please
> to tramp around among the Britons
> or in Scythian frosts to freeze.

Hadrian wrote back, teasing the poet for his lazy life in Rome:

> And I don't want to be Florus, please,
> to tramp around in pubs and bars,
> and get myself infested with fleas.

Hadrian preferred ordinary folk to the pompous aristocrats of Rome. He enjoyed talking to common men and even went to the public baths.

Anonymous, *Augustan History*, 390 CE

> Once Hadrian saw a veteran, whom he knew from the army, rubbing his back against the wall. Hadrian asked the man why he used the marble to scrape himself. When Hadrian found out that the old soldier had no slave, the emperor gave him three slaves and the money to support them.

Hadrian was friendly with his soldiers, but he also knew that strict discipline was important if battles were to be won. After traveling to a military fort in North Africa, Hadrian made a speech to the troops. He praised the cavalrymen for digging trenches in a single day and for building a stone wall in record time. To the auxiliary troops, he said: "You threw your short, stiff javelins gracefully, and several of you hurled your long lances equally well. You mounted your horses nimbly. . . . If anything were lacking, I would have noticed it, . . . but you have pleased me . . . in the entire exercise."

Inscription from Africa, 128 CE

Hadrian wanted to avoid unnecessary wars. He pulled the imperial forces back from some of the farthest frontiers so that the empire's borders could be more easily defended. The greatest evidence of his frontier policy is Hadrian's Wall, which runs for 74 miles across northern England from the North Sea to the Irish Sea. It wasn't intended to keep barbarians completely out of the empire—barbarians lived on both sides of the frontier and moved back and forth across it for trade. But the Wall prevented a massive invasion and protected the soldiers from snipers. With watchmen

GETTING CLEAN AND BEAUTIFUL

One of the many jobs that a slave performed in ancient Rome was scraping sweat and dirt from his master's back when he went to the public baths. The slave would use a curved blade called a strigil. Roman ladies used to collect the scraped-off mixture of oil, sweat, and dirt from athletes and gladiators. They used it for their facials.

Hadrian's great wall ran 74 miles across northern England. The soldiers stationed there thought it was the worst of all assignments: far too cold and much too far from Rome.

CARE PACKAGE FROM HOME

In war or in peace, certain things are necessary. Archaeologists have found this letter on papyrus sent to an unknown soldier in Britain: "I have sent you . . . socks (undorum) from Sattua, two pairs of sandals (solearum duo), and two pairs of underpants (subligariorum duo). . . ."

pagus = "village"
When the Christian religion was new, the Christians looked down on anyone who still believed in the traditional gods of ancient Rome, such as Jupiter, Venus, and Mars. They called such a person a "pagan"—it was a 1st-century version of "hick" or "country bumpkin."

standing guard at every mile, the soldiers could move around safely within the camps.

Archaeologists are still exploring the remains of the forts that Hadrian built along the length of the Wall. Among their finds have been iron pots and pans, spears, and thousands of nails. They've also discovered the remains of huge buildings used for storing grain. (Tons of grain were needed—the soldiers ate bread three times a day.) One of the most surprising discoveries is a sort of postcard made from a thin piece of wood. An invitation to a woman's birthday party is scratched on its surface.

Hadrian was a great builder in other ways as well. He designed an enormous villa for himself, 20 miles outside Rome. The emperor created pools, cool underground caves, and a private study on a small island surrounded by a moat. On the property are baths, libraries, sculpture gardens, and theaters. Each building is a copy of some place that Hadrian admired during his travels abroad, such as the Painted Stoa (a covered porch) where the philosopher Socrates once taught in Athens. Though parts of his extravagant retreat have disappeared, much of it can still be seen today.

Hadrian also built the Pantheon, a temple dedicated to the worship of all the gods. Until 1958, its dome was the biggest concrete span ever built. It rises 142 feet high and represents the dome of heaven.

How did the Pantheon survive when so many other ancient buildings in the city were destroyed? The answer is that it was re-used, taken over by the Catholic Church in 608 CE. When the Catholic bishop of Rome, also called the pope, consecrated it as a Christian church, he renamed it the Church of St. Mary of the Martyrs.

In order to make it holy, every Catholic church had to have some relic of a saint, such as a bone, a tooth, or perhaps a piece of clothing. So, since the Pantheon had originally been dedicated to **pagan** gods, the pope wanted to make sure that the "new" church would be holy enough to overcome its "unholy" past. According to the church records, 124 wagonloads of bones from the catacombs—the burial ground of early Christians—were brought to the

At his estate in the hills, Hadrian copied his favorite buildings from around the Roman world—a Disneyland for an emperor. This pool copies a canal in Egypt.

Pantheon for its consecration. The building remained a church until the 20th century, when it became a museum.

Another of Hadrian's buildings looms beside the Tiber River. It is the Castel Sant'Angelo ("Castle of the Holy Angel") that Hadrian intended to be his tomb. In the Middle Ages it was turned into a fortress. Popes sometimes used it as a safe and secret hiding place. It's now a museum of medieval weapons.

Hadrian was perhaps the most brilliant and talented man ever to sit on the throne of the Roman Empire. But because the senators never trusted him, they refused to declare him a god after his death, as was usually the case with emperors. However, Hadrian's successor, Antoninus Pius, insisted on making Hadrian a god. He built the Temple of the Deified Hadrian. Antoninus was called "pious" (good or devout) because of the honor he paid to his predecessor, Hadrian.

CHAPTER 21

MAGIC AND THE CULTS OF THE NEAR EAST

NEW RELIGIOUS IDEAS

PLINY THE ELDER, CURSE FOUND IN NORTH AFRICA, CATO, SUETONIUS, AND LIVY

Pliny the Elder, *Natural History*, 77 CE

"Superstition" comes from *superstitio,* meaning a belief in charms, omens, and supernatural powers. The 1st-century writer Seneca said, "*religio* honors the gods, *superstitio* wrongs them"

Pliny the Elder, the scientist who took notes while Mt. Vesuvius erupted, advised women to tie a spider to their bodies to prevent an unwanted pregnancy. He also claimed that "people who are not present at a conversation can know by the ringing in their ears that the talk is about them." This, he declared, was "an accepted belief." Another word of wisdom from Pliny was this: "Cutting your hair on the seventeenth day or the twenty-ninth day of the month prevents baldness—and headaches too."

If an educated man like Pliny held such beliefs, it's safe to say that the Romans of his day were **superstitious.** Most people believed in witches, and magic was popular, especially among the lower classes. And almost everyone feared the evil eye—believing that certain people could bring misfortune or even death to someone else just by looking at him. They thought that the evil eye could change the weather, kill crops, or make a healthy person grow suddenly ill.

Rome's port teems with sailors and ships; a fire burns atop the lighthouse. Near the bearded sea god Neptune is a huge eye to ward off danger. (There's a similar eye on the U.S. one-dollar bill.)

People tried to protect themselves against this mysterious power with special spells and charms, including paintings and bracelets, to ward off the evil spirits.

If a Roman wanted to call down the forces of evil on his enemy, he might write curse words on a stone tablet or a thin sheet of lead. Often the curse contained nonsense words that didn't actually mean anything—words like *abracadabra,* for example. And sometimes the tablet would show a sketch of the hated person's face. After sticking long nails through the tablet, the curse-giver would bury the tablet in order to bring his victim closer to the dark spirits of the underworld.

Chariot drivers were especially superstitious. They cared a lot about their races—not only for the fame and money, but also because they risked their lives every time they thundered into the arena. So they sought supernatural aid to bring victory to themselves and defeat to their opponents. Fans of chariot teams also used superstitious means of bringing victory to their favorites—not just out of loyalty but because they stood to win large sums by betting. Competitors and fans of different teams were sometimes bitter enemies, and they tried to draw down curses upon each other. This curse was found in North Africa, an area well known for its racehorses:

> I call upon you, O demon, whoever you are, and ask that from this hour, from this day, from this moment, you torture and kill the horses of the Green and White teams, and that you kill and completely crush the charioteers Clarus, Felix, Primulus, and Romanus. . . . Leave not a breath in their bodies.

“ Curse found in North Africa, no date

Sometimes people stuck needles into clay dolls that represented their enemies. A Roman man might do this to punish his former girlfriend, for example. But that same man might use a different, friendlier spell to make sure that his new girlfriend would love him forever. Magic was a way of controlling people; it was a way of making the world safer and life more satisfying.

Supernatural beliefs were everywhere in Roman society. Even practical old Cato, the traditional, simple-living sena-

A woman dances wildly to honor Dionysius, the god of wine—in Rome, he's called Bacchus. This wall painting can still be seen in the Villa of the Mysteries, near Pompeii.

tor, believed in magical chants. Here is his cure for a dislocated joint or a broken bone. First, "take a hollow green stem and split it down the middle. Have two men hold it against their hips. Begin to chant: '*motas vaeta daries astatares dissunapiter.*'" (These are nonsense words.) The next step was to split the reed in half and attach it to the injured arm or leg. He advised more chanting every day until the wound was completely healed.

“ Cato, *On Agriculture*, about 160 BCE

Many Romans, especially aristocrats, found the study of astrology more believable than curses, omens, and magical charms. It seemed much more scientific and rational, so they often turned to astrologers for advice. Astrologers, then as now, attempted to find answers to life's mysteries in the movements of the planets and the positions of the stars. They used careful observation and mathematics to analyze and predict the heavenly movements that would explain the present and the future.

Many ancient Romans depended upon astrology in their daily lives and as they made decisions. Should I plant my grain field tomorrow, a farmer might ask, or should I wait until the new moon rises in the sky? A wealthy widow might consult an astrologer to find out about her love life: Does Cassius truly love me or does he just want control of my land? An old man might ask an astrologer to help him figure out why he and his son can't seem to get along together.

For the Romans, religion was like a huge basket filled with gods. They had their traditional gods—like Jupiter, Venus, and Mars, plus their lesser gods such as Ceres and Bacchus. But they kept adding to the collection. They adopted the gods of their enemies and the peoples whom they conquered. They often worshiped an emperor after his death. Octavian—later called Augustus—began the practice. After the murder of Julius Caesar, he declared his adopted father a god and called himself the "son of the god." The Senate proclaimed Augustus a god after his death. At his funeral, "an official actually swore that he had seen Augustus's spirit soaring up to heaven through the flames." Vespasian even made a joke about it. As he lay dying, he said, "Alas, I think I am becoming a god."

“ Suetonius, *Life of Augustus,* 130 CE

“ Suetonius, *Life of Vespasian,* 130 CE

Rome's early religion was connected to a particular place. People worshiped the spirits that lived in *this* river or *that* woodland. Certain gods protected particular cities. But as the empire grew, soldiers, slaves, and merchants brought new ideas and new beliefs to Rome. And the Romans themselves began to travel more. They encountered new religions that promised great rewards, such as life after death. They found gods that were not tied to a single city—gods that they could worship wherever their followers gathered to pray.

Gradually, new religions came to Rome from the eastern Mediterranean. Cybele was the first Asian goddess to reach Rome and become popular (about 200 BCE). The people of Asia Minor (modern Turkey) honored her as the Great Mother of the gods. Cybele's story begins in summer. The goddess is in love with a young shepherd named Attis. But Attis becomes ill. And when he dies, Cybele is overcome with grief. The world goes cold as she mourns. But then a miracle happens. Each year in the spring, Attis comes back to life. This story explained the mystery of the seasons—it explained the cold of winter and the blossoming of new life in spring. The Romans loved Cybele and added her to their collected gods and goddesses.

In 205 BCE, when Rome was still frightened of the Carthaginian general Hannibal, government leaders brought a huge black stone from Asia Minor. This rock, a meteorite, was believed to be Cybele herself. The Romans thought that if they brought the goddess into Rome, she would protect them from their enemies. Livy wrote: "The whole city turned out to meet her, and incense was placed in front of doorways along the way. . . . Matrons carried her into the Temple of Victory . . . and the day became an annual festival."

Livy, *From the Founding of the City*, 25 BCE

In Asia, Cybele's worshipers celebrated the coming of spring with wild dancing and self-mutilation. The Roman version of this religion was calmer. But even in Rome, Cybele's worshipers sacrificed bulls in her honor. And priests sprinkled her worshipers with bull's blood as they prayed so that they, like Attis, might be reborn.

ferre = "to give birth"
A woman who is fertile is able to have children. And a field that is fertile can produce crops. Fertility means that life will go on: babies will be born and there will be grain for people to eat.

Isis was an ancient Egyptian **fertility** goddess whose worship spread across the Mediterranean. The worship of Isis was also about death and rebirth. According to legend, Isis's husband was murdered and his body cut into pieces. But each spring, Isis was believed to gather up the scattered parts of her husband's body. With his body parts collected again, he could be reborn. This explained the birth of lambs, the blossoming of flowers, and the return of warm weather.

Isis was popular in Pompeii. Her temple there was rebuilt by Numerius Popidius after an earthquake. The town council was

The goddess Cybele sits on her throne with two pet lions beside her. The "great mother" was brought from Asia to Rome, where her temple was built on the Palatine Hill.

so grateful that they elected him to serve on their council even though he was only six years old. Why would a child be elected to the council? It was just a way of honoring his wealthy father, Numerius. As a freed slave, Numerius himself was not eligible to serve.

Worshipers shook this bronze rattle during religious ceremonies honoring Isis. She became popular not only in Egypt and Italy, but in Roman Britain and Germany, too.

Around 100 CE, the cult of Mithras, a sun god, became popular in Rome. The story of Mithras includes his killing of a bull. And when his followers, called Mithraists, worshiped him, the priests sacrificed a bull on the altar. This religion especially appealed to soldiers, and it spread throughout the military camps of the empire.

Many depictions of Mithras killing the bull have survived. This is because Mithras was often worshiped in caves, and the images were well protected underground. Archaeologists have discovered hundreds of paintings and reliefs in Rome itself, but also in the port city of Ostia in modern-day Germany, and even in London. Unfortunately, no texts written by Mithraists themselves remain to tell us why Mithras sacrificed the bull or what it meant to his worshipers. All we have are descriptions written by Christians who opposed Mithraism. Because Mithraism set a high standard of behavior, it became the strongest rival to Christianity when both religions first began to take root in Roman soil.

CHAPTER 22

TACITUS, SYNESIUS, AND THE GOSPEL OF LUKE

TAXES AND TACTICS IN THE PROVINCES

ADMINISTERING THE EMPIRE

Tacitus, *The Life of Agricola*, 98 CE

"There is no place to flee, even the sea is no longer a safe haven because a Roman fleet threatens us there. . . . They are robbers of the world. . . . They steal, they slaughter, they plunder—and they call it 'Empire.' They make a waste-land and call it 'peace.'"

The Roman historian Tacitus put these harsh words in the mouth of Calgacus, a British war chief. Calgacus is speaking to a crowd of angry provincial soldiers, whipping them up to even greater anger against Rome. Then, in another text, Tacitus provides an answer to Calgacus. He has the Roman general Cerialis tell the grumbling provincials that, without Roman rule, their lives would be far worse. He says that they had suffered constant tyranny and war until they came under Rome's authority. "We have made . . . just one demand: that you pay the costs of keeping the peace here. For peace . . . cannot be kept without troops, and troops cannot be maintained without pay, and pay cannot be found without taxation. . . . You enjoy the benefits of excellent emperors as much as we do."

Tacitus, *Histories*, about 110 CE

Calgacus and Cerialis were real people who lived in the first century CE. But Tacitus made up both speeches to show the feelings of people who hated Rome as well as those who were loyal to the empire. The frustration that bristles in Calgacus's words was real. Many people in the provinces *did* complain bitterly about taxes, forced labor, and the cruelty of their Roman masters. But there is truth in Cerialis's speech too. Native peoples were threatened as much by neighboring tribes as by foreign **enemies.** So when Rome came with its powerful weapons and military know-how, it brought greater safety to peoples all over its massive empire.

"Enemy" comes from the Latin words *in* (not) and *amicus* (friend), meaning "not a friend." The Latin word for enemy is *inimicus.*

Once the Romans conquered a region, they brought in governors and tax collectors. And they usually stationed centurions and soldiers in the newly conquered provinces to keep the peace. Many Roman senators served in the provinces as governors and military commanders.

A third-century CE *relief from Germany shows locals paying their taxes to a Roman official. They don't seem very happy about giving up their hard-earned* denarii.

Every province ruled by Rome needed officials to represent Rome's power and collect money from the people there. But Rome showed its real genius by letting its provincial communities mostly govern themselves. The later emperors often chose local men as governors and commanders in the provinces. This was natural because many of the greatest emperors were provincials themselves, from the Spanish-born Trajan to Constantine, a tough soldier from the Balkans.

Sometimes Rome allowed local kings to keep their thrones, as long as they agreed to follow orders. Fishbourne, near Chichester in England, may have been the seat of a local king who worked for Rome after the conquest of Britain. There, archaeologists have found the remains of a palace with 100 rooms. Many had elaborate mosaic floors. Some of these floors are intact, and visitors can still see them at Fishbourne.

We know that Roman soldiers were stationed at Fishbourne. Archaeologists have found a soldier's helmet and also a little girl's ring, buried long ago. Who was that soldier? Was he a local man or did he come from Rome? And who was the little girl who lost her ring? The king's daughter, perhaps? These are among the many mysteries of history.

For ordinary people living in the provinces, the emperor was just a face on a coin. He played no part in their lives. They were mostly concerned with day-to-day matters: the cruelty of officials, justice in the courts, and the price of bread. These were the basics: the things that made them content and peaceable or miserable and rebellious. If taxes

THE SIZE OF AN EMPIRE

The Roman Empire stretched 2,600 miles east to west (from Spain to Syria) and 2,000 miles north to south (from Britain to southern Egypt)—about the same size as the United States. But the empire, measured that way, includes a lot of water (the Mediterranean) as well as the uninhabited Sahara Desert of North Africa.

A man jumps aboard a crowded ship to escape sharp-toothed creatures swimming in the Nile River. The Romans enjoyed using Egyptian settings in their art, especially after Cleopatra's defeat.

were too high, they blamed the tax collector. If laws were harsh, they blamed the local governor, not the emperor. The fourth-century CE philosopher Synesius explains: "The emperor and his friends . . . are just names to us. People know well enough that there will always be an emperor. We are reminded of that every year by the tax-collectors. But who the emperor may be, the people have no clear idea."

“ Synesius, *Letters*, about 400 CE

Thousands of Roman soldiers and officials were assigned to the far-flung provinces, and all had to be paid. There was only one way to pay so many men, and that was through taxation, as Cerialis said. Millions of people regularly paid taxes to Rome, and the system worked well for centuries.

Rome's census takers listed the names of everyone in the empire. They also recorded information about each person's property. And taxes were based on these lists. A person with a lot of property paid more than someone who owned very little.

“ Luke, New Testament

Everyone in the empire was required to register in his hometown. Rome's best-known census was the one that

This wooden tablet is coated with wax so that messages can be written with sharpened sticks and later rubbed off. Though similar to school tablets, this one belonged to a Roman tax collector in London.

Augustus was said to have ordered. "In those days, a command went out from Caesar Augustus that all the world should be registered. . . . All went to their own towns to be enrolled. Joseph also went from the town of Nazareth in Galilee to Judea, to the city of David called Bethlehem."

People must have complained about the census—for some, it meant a journey during the winter months. But few dared to disobey the commands of mighty Rome.

In 71 CE, the Emperor Vespasian chose his trusted general Agricola as governor of Britain. Agricola pushed Rome's borders further north, established its control in Wales, and led an invasion into Scotland. Agricola encouraged the building of temples, courthouses, and private homes in his adopted region. He offered an education to the sons of native chiefs and governed with such fairness that, in time, the British leaders began to study and speak Latin. Archaeologists have found inkwells, parchment, and wax tablets among the remains of Roman schools in Britain.

Britons began to imitate the fashions of Rome. Men wore togas. Women wore makeup, using chalk to powder their faces, ashes for mascara, and **ocher** to color their lips. Britons welcomed the towns that Rome built. Each of these "modern" towns had a forum with shops, public baths, a town hall, and a place for games and shows. Gradually, Britons began to think of themselves as Roman. But the Britons and other provincials didn't just copy Roman customs. They usually created a mixture of local and Roman culture.

"Ocher" comes from the Latin word *ochra,* which means yellow. Ocher is a type of clay, which can be either yellow or red. Women used the red variety as lipstick.

By 212 CE, all Britons except slaves were citizens of the empire. Not only Britons, but also Germans, Palestinians, Celts, Greeks, and the peoples of Gaul belonged to the

This graceful Roman aqueduct, the Pont du Gard *("bridge over the river Gard") soars high over the river as it brings water to the city of Nimes in southern France.*

Roman Empire at the height of its power. Dozens of languages and dialects were spoken among them. And all of these free provincials became Roman citizens. This process of bringing everyone in helped to make Rome successful in ruling its huge empire.

Just as Rome absorbed much from its provinces, Rome's language, technology, and customs fell on the native cultures of the provinces like rain on thirsty soil. Long after the Roman Empire became weak, its influence remained strong in the provinces that it had helped to shape.

CHAPTER 23

ONE GOD OR MANY?

THE JEWS OF THE ROMAN EMPIRE

“ THE BOOKS OF GENESIS AND EXODUS, THE FIRST BOOK OF MACCABEES, AND THE GOSPEL OF MATTHEW

The emperor Vespasian's son Titus stormed Jerusalem with a Roman army in 70 CE. A Jewish army defended the city. The slaughter on both sides was terrible, but Titus finally defeated the Jews. The Romans destroyed the Jewish Temple, leaving only one wall standing. Many of the Jews who survived were sold into slavery. The defeat was a crushing blow to Jews throughout the Roman world. Those living away from Jerusalem were no longer allowed to send money to Jerusalem for sacrifices at the Temple. Instead they were forced to send this money to the temple of Jupiter in Rome.

Even though the Jews had been badly defeated in Jerusalem, some rebels escaped to Masada, a steep rock fortress 1,700 feet above the Dead Sea. There, the Jews were almost unreachable, but the Romans didn't give up. They built a huge ramp out of dirt—

Roman soldiers carry treasures stolen from the Jewish Temple. In this detail from the triumphal Arch of Titus, the sacred menorah is taken from Jerusalem.

A sad Jewish slave sits on the ground beneath a palm tree. Is he thinking of his homeland? The face of Vespasian, the emperor who conquered Jerusalem, appears on the other side of the coin.

it took them six months to complete it. But when the Romans finally reached the fortress, the rebels set fire to their own buildings. And all but two women and five children committed suicide.

How had the Romans and the Jews come to such violent conflict? The battle against the Romans was not the first time that the Jews had suffered for their faith, their laws, and their ancient traditions.

According to Jewish scripture, God created light, earth, oceans and rivers, fish, birds, animals, and human beings: both women and men. God's work of creation took six days. "Thus the heavens and the earth were finished, and all their multitude. . . . On the seventh day, God finished the work that he had done, and he rested. . . ." Following God's pattern of work and rest, the Jewish people set aside the seventh day of each week as a holy day. They called this day the Sabbath.

“ Genesis, Hebrew Bible

Ever since the Hebrew King Solomon's time, the people of Jerusalem knew that when they heard three sharp blasts on a ram's horn, the Sabbath was beginning. The sound came at sunset on Friday from the top of the temple that Solomon had built around 950 BCE. For 24 hours from that moment, the Jews would do no work. They didn't cook—food had to be prepared the day before. They were not allowed even to peel a piece of fruit. A girl would not braid her hair. A boy would not light a fire, even on a cold day. The fire had to be started the day before. People couldn't write anything down on that day, and they were allowed to walk only short distances. A mile was too far. And they couldn't carry anything, not even a handkerchief. Some Jews still follow these strict rules today.

Jewish law, found in the Hebrew Bible, set out strict rules for daily life. For example, Jews were not allowed to eat pork, horse, rabbit, or any shellfish such as shrimp. Even acceptable food, such as beef, had to be slaughtered in a certain way to keep the animal from suffering more than necessary. Dairy foods could not be mixed with meat. Such a combination would not be **kosher.** Even today, a kosher cook uses separate pots, pans, plates, knives, spoons, and forks for different food groups. An observant Jew would much rather go hungry than eat non-kosher food.

"Kosher" is a Hebrew word meaning "fit for use" and is usually applied to Jewish laws about food.

The Jews' practices and beliefs made them different from other ancient peoples, most of whom were polytheists—believers in many gods. The Jewish people were monotheists. They believed in one God: **Yahweh.** They made their sacrifices only to him. For them, it would be a sin to worship the many state gods of Rome—Jupiter, Juno, Venus, or Mars. They also refused to bow down to a Roman emperor and call him a god. How could they? Worship of any other god would break the first and greatest of Yahweh's commandments: "You shall have no other gods except me." According to the stories in the Hebrew Bible, Moses—an early Jewish leader—received a set of laws directly from Yahweh, who wrote them on two stone tablets. These Ten Commandments were important to the Jewish people when they established the state of Israel about 1000 BCE, when King David united the Jewish tribes under his rule. And when his son Solomon built the temple in Jerusalem, it became the center of Jewish

"Yahweh" is the Hebrew people's name for God. "Jehovah" is a later Christian form of the same name.

“ Exodus, Hebrew Bible

Jewish pilgrims still flock to the Wailing Wall in Jerusalem, the only part of the temple that was left after it was destroyed in 70 CE.

THE JEWISH JOURNEY

1200 BCE
Moses leads the Jews out of Egypt

1000 BCE
King David creates Jewish state of Israel

950 BCE
King Solomon builds the temple

587 BCE
Babylonians destroy temple and exile Jews

538 BCE
Returning Jews build second temple

164 BCE
Judas Maccabeus defeats Antiochus; establishes Hanukkah

40–4 BCE
Reign of King Herod

70 CE
Romans destroy the second temple

135 CE
Final Jewish revolt; Diaspora of Jews

religion for more than a thousand years. But in the sixth century BCE, the king of Babylon destroyed the temple and drove many Jews into exile. Later King Cyrus of Persia allowed the Jews to return to Jerusalem and helped to rebuild their Temple. The most devoted Jews moved back to Judea, settling in or near Jerusalem. Their lives revolved around the temple, its rituals, worship, and rules. Gradually, there came to be two very different kinds of Jews: temple Jews and the Jews of the Diaspora. The Diaspora Jews were those Jews who scattered and settled all over the eastern Mediterranean world. They were much less strict than temple Jews and often adopted non-Jewish customs and beliefs.

Over the centuries, people sometimes despised and persecuted the Jews because they were different. But others admired them for their high moral standards and strong beliefs. It all depended upon who was in power.

When Antiochus IV became King of Syria in 175 BCE, the Jews once again lost their primary place of worship. Antiochus treated the Jews as his enemies. For him, "different" meant suspicious—dangerous. Antiochus wanted the Jews to be more like Greeks, so he tried to keep them from practicing their religion. He looted the Temple in Jerusalem, stealing the golden altar, candlesticks, and other precious treasures. He even built an altar to Zeus in the ancient temple and sacrificed swine (pigs and hogs) there. The Jewish people were shocked and horrified to have Yahweh's temple fouled by the worship of a pagan god. And the sacrifice of swine made it even worse. According to Jewish laws, pork was unclean.

Antiochus tried to force the Jews to sacrifice swine every day, not only in Jerusalem but in small towns and villages as well. If people refused, the king ordered them to be beaten, tortured, and sometimes crucified.

In 164 BCE, a wealthy landowner named Judas Maccabeus took a stand against Antiochus. He and his four brothers overthrew the idol altar and escaped into the desert. Then they gathered an army of faithful Jews who rose up against the king and defeated him. They cleansed the city, making Jerusalem Jewish again, not Greek. They tore down the pagan altar and built a new one. They rebuilt the inside of the Temple and "brought the candle holders, the altar of incense, and the table into the Temple. Then they offered incense on the altar and lit the lamps on the lampstand, and these gave light in the Temple. . . . So they celebrated the dedication of the altar for eight days."

First Book of Maccabees

Every year, the Jewish people celebrate the great victory of Judas Maccabeus during the eight days of Hanukkah, the Festival of Light. The candles in their nine-branched holders, called menorahs, are lit again. The worshipers rejoice and give thanks with songs and the music of harps, cymbals, and lutes.

After his victory, Judas Maccabeus sent ambassadors to Rome. "They . . . entered the senate chamber and said: 'Judas, who is also called Maccabeus, and his brothers, and the Jewish people have sent us to you to establish alliance and peace with you, so that we may be listed as your allies and friends.'"

First Book of Maccabees

Rome recognized the new Jewish state as an ally. But friendship between the two lasted for only 100 years. Pompey conquered the land of Judea in 63 BCE and took control of Jerusalem. Armed and accompanied by soldiers, Pompey marched into the temple and even entered its most secret and sacred space, the Holy of Holies. Only the Jewish High Priest was allowed to enter this room, and even he could go there only once a year. But Pompey went in anyway. He didn't know—or perhaps he didn't care—that he had dishonored the Jews and all that was sacred to them.

Later, when Mark Antony ruled the eastern Mediterranean, he made Judea a **client** kingdom and gave the throne to Herod. This same King Herod appears as a character in the New Testament story about the birth of Jesus.

"Client" comes from the Latin *clinare,* which means "to lean." A client leans on another person or government for protection. Client kings were often native rulers, subject to Rome.

> In the time of King Herod, after Jesus was born in Bethlehem of Judea, Wise Men from the East came to Jerusalem asking, "Where is the child who has been born king of the Jews? For we have seen his star at its rising and have come to pay him homage."

Matthew, New Testament

The towering fortress at Masada, built on steep rocks, was almost unreachable. Its rocky site allowed a small group of determined Jews to hold out against their powerful Roman attackers.

The Jewish people feared and hated Herod throughout his 33 year rule—from 37 BCE until 4 BCE. This cruel king, who was only half Jewish, did very little to make himself liked or accepted by his subjects. He did convert to Judaism and followed some of its rules—for example, he didn't eat pork. But he didn't really sympathize with the beliefs of the Jews. He tried to force Greek and Roman culture on them. He had Greek lettering stamped on their coins. He put on gladiatorial games, which sickened Jews, and built temples to celebrate the worship of Rome's emperor-gods.

After Herod's death, Judea became a Roman province, and the resentment that had been bubbling during Herod's reign boiled over. The Zealots, a group of Jewish extremists, stirred up the people's passion for freedom. After decades of unrest, a full-scale rebellion finally erupted during Nero's reign. He sent four Roman legions to crush the uprising. Vespasian led the Roman forces, but the Jews were not easily defeated.

After years of war and the destruction at Masada in 73 CE, Israel was in ruins. With the temple gone, priests no longer led the Jewish people, and the traditional sacrifices were no longer allowed. But under the leadership of Yohanan Ben Zaccai, the Jews continued to study their ancient texts and practice their rituals. Rabbis (teachers) became the new community leaders, and the tradition of Rabbinic Judaism began. The Jews still practice this form of Judaism today.

The Jews made only one more attempt to rebel against Roman power. Simon Bar-Kochbar organized a Jewish army against Hadrian, but he was defeated in 135 CE. The Jews who survived scattered throughout the Roman Empire. Jewish communities in Alexandria and Rome now centered around synagogues. Wherever Jewish people lived, they cherished their traditional ideas, books, beliefs, and music. But there was never again a Jewish state until the establishment of modern Israel in 1948.

CHAPTER 24

FROM JESUS TO CONSTANTINE

THE RISE OF CHRISTIANITY

“ THE GOSPELS OF LUKE AND MATTHEW; THE BOOKS OF ISAIAH, ZECHARIAH, AND MICAH; TACITUS; AND EUSEBIUS

Like most Jewish parents in Judea, Mary and Joseph took their firstborn son, Jesus, to the Temple in Jerusalem so that they could present him to God. Following the law, “they offered a sacrifice . . . to the Lord: ‘a pair of turtledoves or two young pigeons.’” But then, according to the Gospel of Luke, a strange thing happened. While Mary and Joseph were in the Temple, an old man named Simeon came up to them and took the baby in his arms. Simeon had long believed that God wouldn’t let him die until he had seen the one who would save Israel from its enemies. Seeing the infant Jesus made Simeon incredibly happy. This child, he believed was the one. He praised God, saying that now he could die in peace because “these eyes of mine have seen the Savior . . . the glory of your people Israel.”

“ Luke, New Testament

“ Luke, New Testament

The Jewish people had suffered again and again during their long history. They had been captives, slaves, and finally the conquered subjects of Rome. But their prophets—those who spoke for God—promised that someday God would send them a great king to free them from enemy rule. This king would be the Messiah, the savior of the Jewish people.

The prophet Isaiah gave these words to the Hebrew god, Yahweh: “Here is my servant. . . . I have put my spirit upon him; he will bring forth justice to the nations. . . . He will not grow faint or be crushed until he has established justice in the earth.” The King was coming. But what would he be like?

“ Isaiah, Hebrew Bible

Although many Jews expected the Messiah to be a warrior king, Zechariah said that the Savior would be a humble man. “See, your king comes to you, triumphant and victorious is he, humble . . . and riding on a colt. . . . And he shall command peace to the nations.” The prophet Micah wrote that the Messiah would be born in Bethlehem. “But you, O

“ Zechariah, Hebrew Bible

“ Micah, Hebrew Bible

70 YEARS LATER

The birth, life, teachings, and death of Jesus are described in the Christian New Testament. But no records written during Jesus' lifetime mention any of these events. The historian Tacitus was the first Roman writer to mention the Christians, 70 years after the death of Jesus.

Bethlehem . . . from you shall come forth . . . one who is to rule in Israel."

According to ancient writings, a large, bright star would appear in the nighttime sky when the Messiah was about to be born. And in his story about Jesus' birth, Matthew describes exactly that. He tells how wise men (probably philosophers or astrologers) followed a brightly shining star to Jerusalem. Then, not knowing exactly where to find the infant king, the travelers went to King Herod's palace and asked. It was the logical place to look. But when Herod heard the question, he was scared. Who was this newborn king who threatened his throne? Herod was taking no chances: he ordered the slaughter of all the newborn babies in Bethlehem! But Mary and Joseph managed to escape with their baby to Egypt where they lived safely until Herod's death.

When Jesus grew to manhood, he chose twelve disciples—close, devoted followers—to help him in his work. Then he began to preach, teach, and work wonders in the villages and synagogues near the Sea of Galilee. (Many wonder-workers and healers traveled from place to place in those days.) Jesus didn't challenge Jewish law, but he did see himself as the King of the Jews. He wasn't a military leader or an organizer. He was a peacemaker and healer. People flocked to see him and hear him speak. He preached to peasants and fishermen. And his message was a simple one about God's love. Later, his followers wrote down the stories of his life—what he taught and what he did.

In his gospel, Matthew records a sermon that Jesus preached early in his ministry. It's called the "Sermon on the Mount" because he preached it, sitting on a hillside, to the people who had gathered there to hear him. It contains some of his most important teachings. Each sentence begins with the word "blessed," which means holy as well as blissfully happy.

" Matthew, New Testament

Blessed are the poor in spirit, for theirs is the
kingdom of heaven.
Blessed are they that mourn, for they shall be comforted.

> Blessed are the meek, for they shall inherit the earth.
> Blessed are those who hunger and thirst after justice,
> for they shall have their fill.
> Blessed are the merciful, for they shall receive mercy.
> Blessed are the pure of heart, for they shall see God.
> Blessed are the peacemakers, for they shall be called
> children of God.

These sayings, called the Beatitudes, emphasize values that were very different from those that the Romans honored—with their many gods and their pride in riches. But Jesus didn't encourage people to rebel against Rome. He even advised them to pay their taxes faithfully: "Give unto Caesar that which is Caesar's, and unto God that which is God's."

“ Matthew, New Testament

The Beatitudes were different from traditional Jewish teachings as well. And this made enemies for Jesus, too. Justice played an important role in traditional Jewish teachings. But Jesus taught a message of forgiveness. "You have heard it said, 'An eye for an eye, and a tooth for a tooth.' But I say to you . . . if anyone strikes you on the right cheek, turn the other cheek as well." The religious leaders of the Temple did not believe that Jesus was the Messiah. And they were afraid that his teachings would weaken their power among the people.

“ Matthew, New Testament

The Jews of Jesus' day knew the law: "You shall love the Lord your God with all your heart, . . . and your neighbor as yourself." According to Luke, Jesus was asked, "Who is my neighbor?" Jesus answered with the parable of the Good Samaritan. In this story, a man is attacked, robbed, and brutally beaten. Two of his own countrymen see the man lying on the side of the road, but neither one stops to help. The wounded man is saved by the kindness of a foreigner, a Samaritan. Jesus was saying that neighbors are those who show kindness to one another, regardless of family, race, or group.

“ Luke, New Testament

After three years of teaching, preaching, and healing the sick, Jesus was arrested by his enemies and brought before a Roman official, Pontius Pilate, for trial. Pilate knew that Jesus wasn't guilty of any crime under Roman law. But to

Jesus' mother, Mary, with Joseph standing behind her, has just put her newborn son into Simeon's arms. The parents listen, amazed, as the old man praises God for the gift of this child.

keep peace with local religious leaders, he ordered that Jesus be crucified between two common criminals.

After his death on the cross, Jesus was buried in a stone tomb and a huge rock was rolled against the door. His disciples and other followers believed that, after three days in the tomb, Jesus rose from the dead. After he was taken into heaven by God, the disciples, led by a fisherman named Peter, began to preach about Jesus—that he had risen from the dead and that he would come again at the end of the world.

Believers gathered in closely knit communities, and the leader of each community was called a bishop. Although Jesus' followers feared persecution from the Roman authorities, they convinced many others that Jesus was the Savior. They called him "Christ," the Greek word for Messiah.

Most of the early disciples didn't go very far from Judea and the nearby Jewish communities in Syria. One of them, however, spread the message of Jesus into the far reaches of the empire.

Saul was the son of a Jewish merchant in the city of Tarsus. He was also a Roman citizen. Educated in the Greek classics, he studied the Hebrew Bible in Jerusalem and developed a hatred for the new Christian religion. Saul persecuted Christians whenever he could. One day, he was riding to Damascus to arrest the Christians there and take them to Jerusalem in chains. According to the New Testament *Acts of the Apostles,* he was suddenly struck by a vision of Jesus. He fell from his horse and was blind for three days. When Saul's sight returned, he became—to the amazement of Jews and Christians alike—Jesus' most loyal and eager follower. He changed his name and his whole life. Saul became Paul: believer, preacher, and Christian writer.

Paul was determined to preach the Gospel of Jesus to people everywhere. He brought Jesus' simple message from the countryside to the big cities where people were more open to new ideas. His preaching took him all over Syria, Asia Minor (modern Turkey), and the ancient cities of Greece. If it hadn't been for him, Christianity might never have spread beyond Palestine. He preached not only to the Jews of the Diaspora, but to others as well. Throughout the Roman Empire, Paul and other missionaries found people who were "God-fearers"—people who admired the high standards of the Jews and appreciated their strong sense of family and community. These people were interested in the message of Jesus, and many became believers.

Paul traveled to Athens, in Greece. There he found an altar dedicated "To the Unknown God." He announced that he had come on behalf of that very god. He preached the good news of a Messiah who promised never-ending life after death. Paul's letters, which were written in Greek, show how he developed the simple teachings of Jesus into a more complicated system of behavior and belief.

Like Jesus, Paul was eventually arrested. He spent more than two years under house arrest, waiting to be tried. His letters, mostly written from prison, were to Christian groups in the different places where he had preached. The letters that survived are among the books of the New Testament. Because Paul was a Roman citizen, he was tried in Rome. During Nero's reign, in the year 62 CE, he became a martyr, which means that he chose to die rather than deny his belief in Jesus Christ.

In 64 CE, Nero was accused of starting the huge fire that burned a large part of Rome. He didn't want the people to turn against him, so he invented charges against the Christians and blamed them for the fire. Many Christians were tortured. Tacitus describes the brutal murders. "People who admitted to their belief were arrested. . . . Mockery was heaped upon them as they were killed. Wrapped in the skins of wild animals, they were torn apart by dogs, or nailed to crosses, or set on fire and burned alive."

Christians were persecuted in the Roman Empire, not because they worshiped Jesus, but because they refused to worship the emperor. This was treason, and the punishment

JESUS THE STORYTELLER

Jesus often told parables—stories that teach a lesson. One of his best known parables is about a rich young man who takes his share of his father's money, leaves home, and spends all the money foolishly. When he is completely broke and hungry, he decides to go home. He plans to beg his father to let him become a servant. But the father welcomes him and throws a party to celebrate his son's homecoming. Jesus said that God is like that father—his love never ends, no matter what.

“ Tacitus, *Annals*, 117 CE

for treason was death. Some governors enforced the punishment, others did not. Many Romans saw Christianity as strange, perhaps dangerous. Christians kept themselves apart from the festivals that honored the traditional gods. They preached that the end of the world was near and that Christ would soon come back to take his followers with him to heaven. Most of the time, Christians practiced their religion in secret in order to survive. They even buried their dead in their own private cemeteries. Today you can visit these tombs, called catacombs, on the outskirts of Rome.

The Christian community grew slowly during the second and third centuries. By 300 CE, only about 5 to 10 percent of the people in the Roman Empire had been converted to Christianity. But the Church had become much more organized. Each city had a bishop. The priests became a separate body of lower-ranking leaders who led the congregations, or groups of believers.

Christian history took a new and important direction in October of 312 CE. A general named Constantine was fighting for control of the Empire. Though his mother had become a Christian, Constantine was devoted to the pagan gods of Rome. On the day before an important battle, he had a vision. According to the historian Eusebius, "he saw with his own eyes . . . a cross of light in the heavens, above the sun, and

“ Eusebius, *Ecclesiastical History*, 325 CE

Christian tombs line the walls of these huge underground rooms, called catacombs, outside the walls of Rome. Pilgrims later came to honor the early Christians buried here.

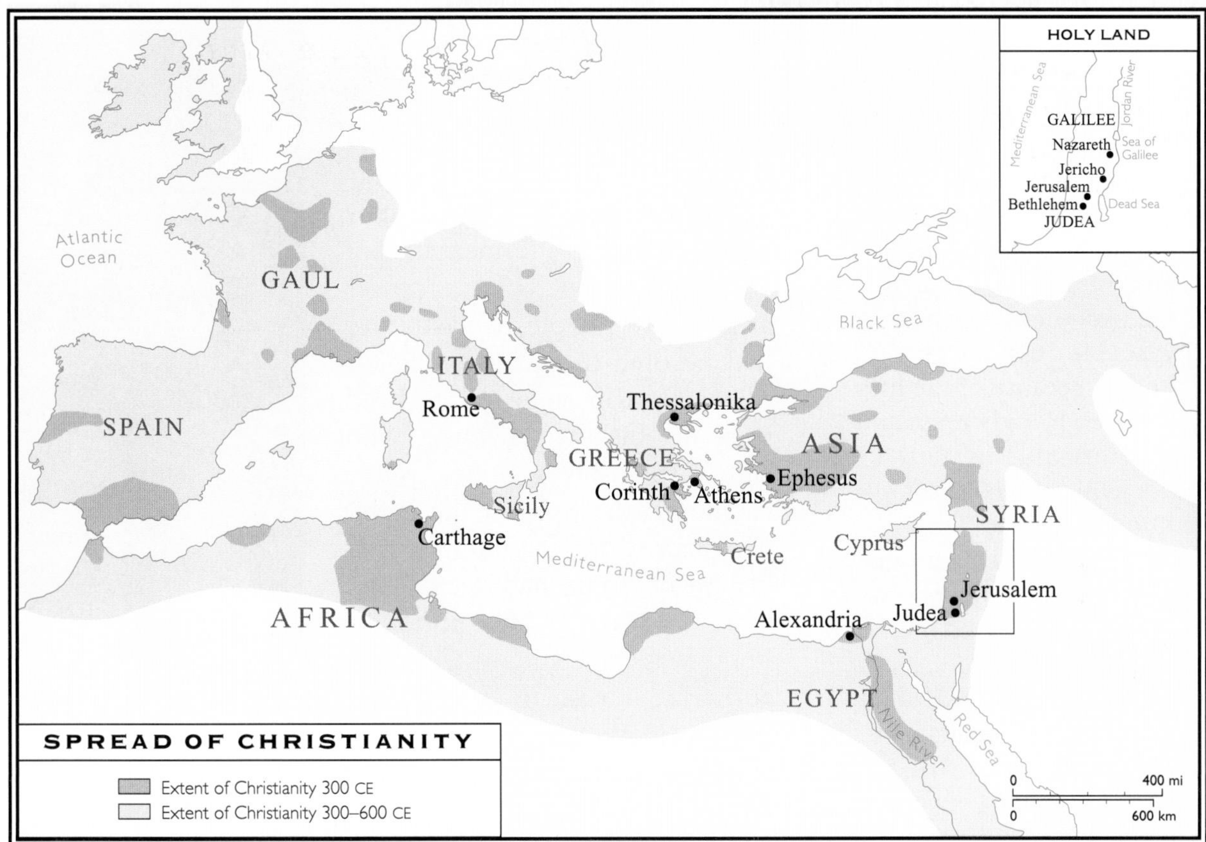

bearing the inscription, 'Conquer by this.' At this sight he himself was struck with amazement, and his whole army also." Later that night Christ appeared to him in a dream. The next day, before the battle began, Constantine ordered his soldiers to paint the first two letters of Christ's name—the Greek letters *chi* and *rho*—on their shields. His army won the battle, and he was sure that Christ had given him the victory. Although Constantine never gave up his pagan gods, he worshiped Christ from that day on.

Constantine became emperor, and his newfound faith completely changed the picture for the Christian community. He ruled that no one should be persecuted for his or her beliefs. He built many churches but he never forced Christianity on his subjects. And although the Roman army and people remained mostly pagan, Christians no longer had to hide their beliefs. Christianity could spread much more quickly.

TELLING TIME

A sixth-century CE monk first figured out the date of Jesus' birth. Unfortunately, the monk made a mistake, and the year he came up with was at least four years off. How do we know? Because of the link between Herod's reign and the story of Jesus' early life. Official records of Rome state that Herod died in 4 BCE. This means that Jesus had to be born before 4 BCE. Based on a study of Christian texts as well as Jewish and Roman documents, scholars now believe that Jesus was born sometime between 6 and 4 BCE.

This enormous head of Constantine, Rome's emperor from 306 to 337 CE, was once part of a 30-foot-high statue. Only the head, arm, and foot have survived.

By the time of Constantine's death in 337 CE, Rome's ancient gods had lost much of their power among the people. Christianity had become the favored religion of the Roman state. At its head were the bishops of Rome, who called themselves popes. They claimed authority over the entire Christian church because the first bishop of Rome had been Peter, Christ's disciple. But although Rome was the center of Christian authority, it was no longer the only capital of the Roman Empire. Now there were two.

Constantine had built a new capital city in Asia Minor in 330 CE. Its name was Constantinople (now Istanbul, Turkey), and Constantine called it "the New Rome." It was not only better placed to fight against Rome's Persian enemies, but Constantine believed he could create a truly Christian capital. He offered special incentives, including free grain, to encourage people to move there. Constantinople became a focus of education and the arts—a magnet for Christian visitors and pilgrims.

CHAPTER 25

ROME'S POWER SLIPS AWAY

THE BARBARIANS

TACITUS, SUETONIUS, LACTANTIUS, AND THE LIFE OF LEO THE GREAT

On September 9 in the year 9 CE, the Roman governor and general Quinctilius Varus led three legions right into the hands—and swords—of their enemies. Narrow ravines forced the Romans to walk in ones and twos, and the army became a string of undefended men. The last soldier was half a day's march from the first. Then a force of Germans, led by a man named Arminius, attacked with surprise and brutal force. Only a few Romans survived.

Six years passed before another Roman army reached the site of the massacre and actually saw the remains. According to Tacitus: "There in the field were . . . the bones of men . . . strewn about or piled in heaps. . . . And so the Roman army, . . . in grief and anger, buried the bones of the three legions. No soldier . . . knew whether he was burying the remains of his kinsman—or those of a stranger."

Tacitus, *The Annals*, 117 CE

How could three Roman legions have been so completely defeated and dishonored? That question tortured the emperor, Augustus Caesar. The emperor was so upset that he didn't shave his beard for three months. He was in mourning. And he raged through the palace screaming, "Varus, give me back my legions!" Great Rome had not suffered such a disaster since Hannibal's victory at Cannae 225 years

Suetonius, *Life of Augustus*, 130 CE

This strong young soldier has been wounded and defeated in battle. The pendant on the dying man's necklace tells us that he is from Gaul.

before. The empire had not only been defeated, it had been shamed. How could this happen? The answer lies in the personalities of the two leaders: Varus and Arminius.

Varus was a successful politician in Rome. His career got a big boost when he married the emperor's great-niece. But imperial connections weren't enough, and Varus was a terrible judge of human nature. When he became the provincial governor over the Germanic tribes, he treated the Germans as though they were slaves of Rome. His attitude infuriated the Germanic tribes and their leader, Arminius.

Unlike Varus, Arminius was smart—and sneaky. With generous doses of flattery, he convinced the governor that the people were happy with his leadership and would obey him, whatever he asked. Varus never questioned the truth of Arminius's smoothly buttered words. So all Arminius had to do was wait—bide his time—until Varus grew careless. And then he set his trap.

THE DIVIDING LINE

In his grief and shock after the defeat of Varus's legion, Augustus pulled his troops back to the Rhine River. To this day, the Rhine marks the border between German-speaking people and those who speak French, a Latin-based language.

Arminius sent Varus a message about a fake uprising and persuaded the governor to lead his troops through a dense forest in order to put down the rebels. Arminius and his men were ready and waiting. They ambushed the Romans, slaughtering not only the soldiers but also their wives, children, and servants. Then they left the bodies to rot and their bones to whiten in the sun. Varus had badly underestimated his enemy. The reasons were partly grounded in the history of relations between Rome and the people it called **barbarians.**

"Barbarian" comes from the Greek word *barbaros*, which means foreigners. When native peoples spoke their languages, the Greeks thought all the words sounded like "bar-bar." The Latin word *barbaria*, meaning "foreign country," comes from the Greek term.

As the Romans expanded their borders into Gaul, Spain, Germany, and Britain, they met peoples who knew nothing of Greek or Roman culture. Though most of these so-called barbarians were Celts or Germans, they didn't share a common culture or language. In fact, they fought with each other more than they fought with the Romans. Since they left no written records of their own, what we know of them comes from archaeological evidence and from Roman descriptions of them.

At first, the Romans were terrified of these rough, uncultured tribes. After all, the Gauls had temporarily captured Rome in 390 BCE. But after Rome had defeated the armies of the Carthaginian general Hannibal and a few

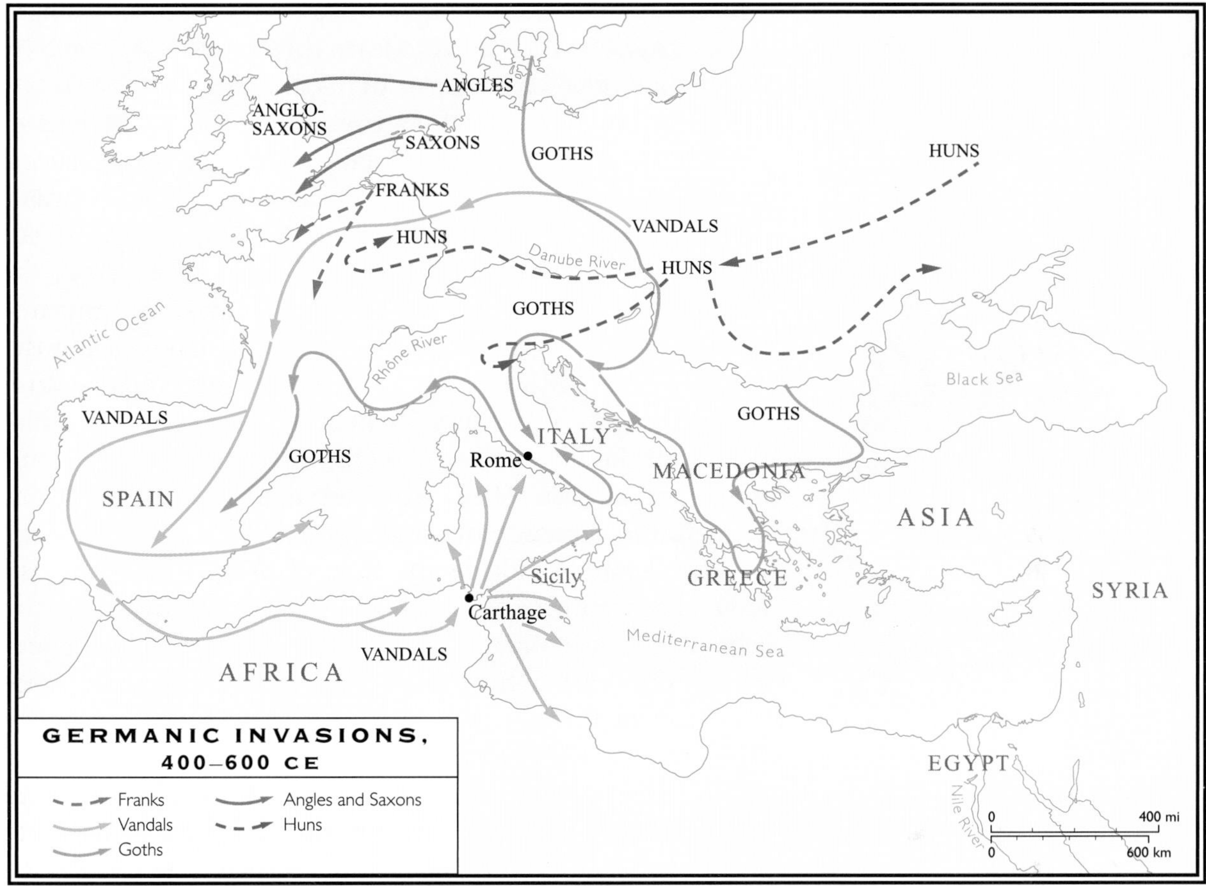

Greek and Asian kings, the Romans felt they had little to fear from the disorganized peoples on their northern borders. For centuries, Roman soldiers were better trained than their enemies. They had sharper spears, stronger swords and armor. And they had powerful machines of war to catapult stones at their enemies and lay siege to their cities.

Roman views of the barbarians changed over time. At first, the Romans considered them all to be savages. The Romans assumed that these unfamiliar peoples were cruel and had no self-control. All barbarians were thought to follow strange practices such as cannibalism. Gradually, the Romans discovered that they were wrong: the provincial peoples were *not* all the same. Some were crude and untrained, but their differing customs and languages did not mean they were all dull

Roman soldiers hold a captured barbarian in this decoration from the marble arch that Constantine built to celebrate his victory in 312 CE.

witted. Some, like Arminius, proved to be shrewd military men. Varus, it seems, failed to learn this crucial lesson, and he paid a high price for the error of his thinking.

In time, Rome's emperors began to recruit barbarians to serve in their armies. Eventually, barbarian generals led Roman armies against other barbarians who tried to move into the empire. Often, these were not invading armies, but hordes of what we now call immigrants.

These peoples came, with their families and animals, from eastern Europe in search of the fertile lands nearer the Mediterranean. Most of them left their native lands because they were hungry and poor, or because they were pushed by other warlike peoples, such as the Huns moving westward from central Asia. Wave after wave of barbarian nations pushed into Roman territory.

Rome fought to stop the flow of peoples who tried to cross the frontiers of the Rhine and Danube rivers. In the second century CE, the emperor Marcus Aurelius spent almost ten years fighting against them. But they kept coming. Late in the fourth century CE, a long drought drove tribes of nomadic horsemen from their homeland in Central Asia. These peoples, whom we call Huns, pushed into Germany. They conquered the peoples already living there and forced them to migrate into the Roman Empire. As one group moved in, another was forced to move out.

One group of Germans, the Goths, marched into Italy in 410 CE. As the Goths came near Rome, the Roman troops panicked and shamefully abandoned the field of battle. The Vestal Virgins managed to save—and bury—the sacred vessels from Vesta's temple. They carried the eternal fires of Vesta to a place of safety beyond the gates of the city. A large part of the population fled across the Tiber River. The Goths ransacked the city, destroying or stealing at will, an event called the "Sack of Rome."

The Sack was a huge shock to the capital city. A barbarian army had not captured mighty Rome in 800 years. (No great city has ever been undefeated for this long.) The idea of *Roma Aeterna*—Eternal Rome—had long been proclaimed by its rulers and celebrated by its writers. The words were stamped on Roman coins. For Rome to be defeated was almost unthinkable. A century earlier, a Christian writer had imagined the fall of Rome and compared it to the end of the world:

> The fall and ruin of the world will soon take place, but nothing . . . is to be feared as long as the city of Rome stands intact. But when the capital of the world has fallen, . . . who can doubt that the end will have come for . . . the whole world?

Lactantius, *Divine Institutes,* 313 CE

Rome's defeat by the Goths was traumatic, but the Goths did not actually destroy the city. Rome survived, and its emperors recovered from the shock. But Rome never again had the power it once had held.

Forty years later, the Huns and their leader Attila "came into Italy, . . . inflamed with fury . . . utterly cruel in inflicting torture." Pope Leo, the supreme leader of the Roman Catholic Church, went to the outskirts of the city to meet the barbarian king. Leo, a gentle old man with gray hair, "begged Attila to spare Rome, saying, 'The Senate and the people of Rome, once conquerors of the world, now conquered, come before you as beggars. . . . The people have felt your punishments. Now as beggars, we ask for your mercy.'"

Anonymous, *The Life of Leo the Great,* after 550 CE

Two angels help Pope Leo convince Attila to show mercy to Rome in this 16th-century painting by the Italian artist Raphael. Scholars now think the pope offered him a huge amount of money to spare the city.

According to the same anonymous source, Attila was moved by Rome's sad plight. He "promised a lasting peace and withdrew beyond the Danube." The Hun warlord had spared Rome, yet the capital was now at the mercy of barbarian lords. It was no longer unbeatable, unbreakable. It was no longer Eternal Rome.

SYMMACHUS AND CASSIODORUS

CHAPTER 26

THE EMPIRE, DIVIDED AND DEFEATED

THE FALL OF ROME

In Plutarch's story about the founding of Rome, the Trojans named their new city for Roma, a rebellious wife who burned the Trojan ships. Centuries later, another writer, Symmachus, gives us another picture of Roma. Now she is an old woman. Speaking to the emperor, Roma says that she is used to being admired and honored. But things have changed, and she is sad. People are following new ways, worshiping new gods.

Symmachus, *Dispatches to the Emperor,* 383 CE

Roma says she is too old to change. She doesn't want to change—and besides, she shouldn't have to at her age. "Best of emperors, fathers of the fatherland, respect my age. . . . Let me enjoy the ancient ceremonies, for I do not regret them. Let me live in my own way, for I am free. This is the religion which made the whole world obedient to my laws. . . . Change in old age is humiliating."

"Horrify" comes from the word *horrificare,* which means to bristle, shake, or be afraid.

Symmachus, a fourth-century CE orator and consul, had always loved Rome as it was before Christianity replaced the traditional gods. But during his lifetime, he had seen Rome change. He was **horrified** when the Christian emperor Gratian took the Altar of Victory out of the Senate house. Augustus himself had placed it there in 30 BCE as a symbol of Rome's good relationship with its ancient gods. Symmachus believed that these same gods had protected Rome and made it glorious. But those gods were doomed. In 392 the emperor Theodosius the Great outlawed pagan worship. Christianity had won against the old gods of Rome.

Rome's glory faded during the fourth and fifth centuries. Historians usually give 476 CE as the date for its fall. But Rome did not fall like an apple from a tree. It was more gradual than that. About 235 CE, after two and a half centuries of stable government, the Roman Empire fell into chaos. Numerous armies declared their generals "emperor," and the Roman legions fought each other instead of defending the frontiers. They named almost 50 emperors during the next 50 years. But fewer than 20 made it to Rome, and not one of them died of natural causes. An extraordinary man named Diocletian finally broke the pattern of violence and restored order to the empire.

Diocletian came from humble beginnings. His father may even have been a freed slave. Although he started at the bottom, Diocletian rose through the ranks and became a general. He served under the emperor Numerian until 284 CE, when Numerian was murdered. When Diocletian murdered the emperor's killer, the army proclaimed him emperor of Rome.

Diocletian was a practical man. He saw how hard it would be to rule such a huge territory. He realized that he needed to reorganize the army and improve tax collecting. Otherwise, how could he pay the army? He decided to divide the empire into two parts with four rulers: two senior emperors (*Augusti*) and two junior emperors (*Caesares*). This tetrarchy ("rule of four") worked pretty well until Diocletian became ill and gave up his power.

The Emperor Hadrian built the Pantheon to honor the gods of ancient Rome. This temple represents the old religion that Roma loved so much. Today, it symbolizes the old and new worlds of Rome—the ancient temple surrounded by modern buildings and the constant buzz of traffic. It's surrounded, yet beautiful; besieged, but still serene.

Jesus' mother, Mary, sits on a throne, holding him as two emperors bring gifts. On the right is Constantine holding a model of the city he founded, Constantinople. On the left, the emperor Justinian brings Jesus a model of the Hagia Sophia.

Warring generals fought for control of the empire until Constantine's victory in 312 CE. Now power shifted to the east. Constantine founded the new capital city of Constantinople in 330 CE. From there, his successors ruled a unified empire until the death of the emperor Theodosius in 395 CE. Then the empire actually split into two parts, with two emperors in two separate capitals: Rome in the west and Constantinople in the east. This made a huge difference and was a major step towards "the fall."

Foreign invasions also contributed to Rome's fall. For a century, barbarians had battered Italy so fiercely that the western emperors had to call their troops back from the provinces. The soldiers were needed at home. Rome pulled the last of its troops from Britain in 407 CE. With the Roman forces gone, the Irish and Scots as well as the barbarian tribes from Germany soon overran the British population. Rome's 400-year rule over Britain had ended. At the same time another German tribe called the **Vandals** devastated Gaul, passed through Spain, and by 429 had established a kingdom in North Africa. Now the barbarians controlled nearly all the western provinces of Rome's once-great empire.

"Vandalism" comes from the name of a Germanic tribe that, like the Goths, invaded Italy. The Vandals were a powerful and destructive tribe; the term "vandalism" means malicious destruction.

Then, in 476 CE, German invaders forced the Roman emperor from his throne. This emperor, Romulus Augustulus, was only 12 years old. And even though he had the names of Rome's first king and its first emperor, he wasn't very impressive. He was a child, and not a strong one. A German named Odoacer became king in his place, and Romulus retired to a house in the country.

Few people living in Rome in 476 CE would have called this event "the Fall of Rome." But later writers and historians saw how important it really was. Looking back, it became clear that Rome was never quite the same after 476 CE.

Most historians agree on the date of Rome's fall, but they have been arguing for centuries about why. Some, agreeing with Symmachus, blamed Christianity. Yet the emperors who ruled in Constantinople were Christian, too, and Constantinople prospered long after 476 CE. The other Roman emperor still ruled there, and although the citizens of Constantinople spoke Greek, they still called themselves Romans. In fact, the eastern capital called itself "Roman" for another 1,000 years.

This domed building in Istanbul was once the Hagia Sophia, the Church of Holy Wisdom, built by Justinian and dedicated in 563 CE. It later became a Muslim mosque and is now a museum.

The cause of Rome's fall has to be something that was true for the Western Empire, but not for the Eastern Empire. One difference between the two empires was geography. The Western Empire had to defend much longer borders. Its troops were spread out, which made them more vulnerable—more easily attacked and defeated. The Eastern Empire had many more people and could support a much larger army. It included the rich lands of Egypt and controlled a lively, moneymaking trade with Arabia, China, and India. Its wealthy cities produced manufactured goods that brought in taxes. Yet Rome frowned on manufacturing and still relied upon agriculture for its income. The landowning aristocrats of Rome made money, but often in corrupt ways. Even more harmful was their use of private armies and political connections to avoid paying taxes.

When the empire actually split, Rome could no longer collect taxes from the wealthy east. Suddenly, there was almost no money coming in. The government in Rome

After the fall of Rome, grass grew up in the Forum and it became a park—cows even grazed there. For a time, it was called campo vaccino, *the "cow pasture."*

grew desperate. It raised taxes and seized crops to feed its army. Hungry farmers joined the foreign invaders. As more and more taxable land fell into the hands of the German invaders, the state budget grew smaller and smaller.

"Magnificent" comes from the words, *magnus* (great) and *facere* (to do, to make).

When the foreign king Odoacer took the throne in Rome, the **magnificent** days of imperial Rome were over. But even the conquering barbarians admired Roman civilization. The German kings not only adopted Christianity but tried to hold on to Rome's glory as well. They paid poets to write hymns in Latin. They borrowed Rome's system of laws and adapted it to fit their own needs. Other Europeans tried to meet the standard set by Rome. As the Gothic king Theodoric liked to say, "an able Goth wants to be like a Roman; only a poor Roman would want to be like a Goth."

“ Cassiodorus, *Variae,* 537 CE

EPILOGUE

THE LEGACIES OF ANCIENT ROME

In many ways, cities and empires are like people. You are the same person you were at age six, but you're also very different. A big event—such as moving to a new city, a divorce in the family, or the birth of a younger brother or sister—may have made a huge difference in your life. But you are still you—the same, yet different.

This could also be said of Rome. Many things changed after 476 CE, but others stayed the same. In the decades after Rome's fall, some Italian cities were abandoned. Grand buildings collapsed. Roman civilization, once so glorious, no longer blanketed the known world. In some places, Roman culture completely disappeared. But the 90 percent of the people who worked on the land went on as they always had. People still lived in the city of Rome. They bought olive oil, grain, wine, sandals, and cloth, using the same coins they had used before. Most government officials stayed the same. And they still conducted their business in Latin.

The first President of the United States, George Washington, is portrayed as the bare-chested Roman god Jupiter. The Presidential feet wear sandals, and his hand holds a Roman sword.

THE BISHOP OF ROME

The Pope of Rome is still the head of the Roman Catholic Church. In "church Latin," the word *papa* means father or daddy. And the English word "pope" comes from *papa*. Once again, Rome's most powerful leader was described as a father.

Rome's civic or state government failed, but its religious government grew stronger than ever. The bishops of Rome, or popes, became the most powerful leaders in the Christian Church. The activities that surrounded the Church made Rome the leading city in Europe for many centuries. For this reason, churchmen, foreign ambassadors, and scholars kept using Latin as their official language for more than 1,000 years.

We find traces of Rome all over Europe, Britain, and the Mediterranean world. Arrow-straight roads, aqueducts, temples, public baths, walls, and fortresses all say: "Rome was here." The use of cement in ancient buildings, such as the huge baths built in Paris, points to Rome as well—the Romans invented the technology for making cement, the main ingredient in concrete. But Rome's influence is not found just in tangible things—things we can touch. Roman ideas of contracts, property, and inheritance form the basis of European—and American—law.

In the 15th century, Italian painters, sculptors, and architects "rediscovered" the art of ancient Rome and Greece. This is what we call the **Renaissance.** During this time of rebirth, Roman domes and Greek columns appeared once again in churches and state buildings all over Europe.

re + *nasci* = "again" + "to be born" "Renaissance" means rebirth—to be born again, or recreated. Whenever something begins to be popular again, it may be called a "renaissance." This old thing that becomes new again can be a style of art, clothing, music . . . even ideas.

Later, in the 18th century, many government buildings and monuments of the newly formed United States of America showed the influence of Greek and Roman art and architecture. The U.S. Capitol, with its gleaming white marble, looks as if it might have been designed for Rome itself. This was no accident. The founding fathers borrowed many ideas from Rome in their search for a balanced democracy. It made sense that their buildings should also echo Rome.

The United States government follows the pattern set by the founders of the Roman republic with a division of power between its two houses: the Senate and the House of Representatives. As in ancient Rome, a system of checks and balances keeps any one branch of the government from having too much power. The French Republic of the 1790s also had a "Senate" and "Assembly" modeled on Rome.

The idea of civic duty is borrowed from Rome as well. When you vote, not too long from now, or serve on a jury, you will be celebrating your Roman heritage. If you take an unpaid office in your town, work in a homeless shelter, or join the volunteer firemen, you will be doing your civic duty. Civic duty takes countless forms. When a football or basketball star visits a children's hospital, the ghost of old Cicero smiles. "The private individual ought . . . to live on fair and equal terms with his fellow citizens . . . and to work for the peace and honor of the state, for such a person we . . . respect and call a good citizen."

“ Cicero, *On Duties*, 44 BCE

Imagine Roma, that legendary spirit of the city, once again. She is old and writing her will, deciding what she will leave to others. To whom will she give her gifts, her legacies? The good news is that Roma named you in her will. And you use her legacies every day of your life.

Many of the books that you read and study are based on Roman tales—the stories of the city's founding, its heroes, its wars, and romances. Shakespeare based many of his plays on Roman comedies. Hundreds of modern books, movies, and plays are also based upon the history of Rome.

Arches, stately columns, and a huge dome mark the U.S. capitol building as a descendant of Roman architecture. The governing system inside also reflects Rome: "the Republic for which it stands."

The Los Angeles Coliseum was built for the Olympic games of 1932 and hosted the 1984 games. Its tall arches echo the original Colosseum (the Latin spelling) in Rome.

Words are among Roma's most generous gifts. It's true that Latin died out as a spoken language long ago. But like a big bag of flour that disappears, only to return as bread, cookies, noodles, and cakes, Latin formed the basis of other languages—Italian, French, Spanish, Catalan, Portuguese, and Romanian. English, too, is enriched by Latin. We use many Latin words in their original forms—words such as **et cetera**, **circus**, **auditorium**, and **video.** Thousands more English words come from Latin—words such as library, nation, factory, and victory. Even "school" comes from the Latin *schola.* And the book you are holding right now is another gift from Roma. It's written with the Roman alphabet.

et + cetera =
"and" + "other things"
circus = "round"
audire = "to hear"
video = "I see"

You'll never escape the influence of ancient Rome—don't even try!

TIMELINE

BCE

1000
Arrival of Aeneas in Italy

900–800
Etruscans appear in northern Italy

800–700
Greeks colonize Sicily and southern Italy; Phoenicians colonize Carthage

753
Romulus founds Rome

753–509
Roman monarchy rules

616–509
Etruscan kings rule Rome

509
Sextus attacks Lucretia; foundation of Roman Republic

509–27
Roman Republic

493
Workers abandon Rome for the first time

475
Horatius defends Rome

458
Cincinnatus defends Rome

450
Workers abandon Rome for the second time; the Senate writes the Twelve Tables

390
Gauls sack Rome

266
Rome conquers Italian peninsula

264–133
Rome fights overseas enemies

264–241
First Punic War

218–202
Second Punic War

197
Rome takes control of Spain

196
Rome defeats Philip of Macedon

164
Judas Maccabeus defeats King Antiochus

146
Greece becomes a Roman province

133–31
Domestic unrest in Rome

133–121
Tiberius and Gaius Gracchi champion the poor

90–88
War of the Allies

73
Spartacus leads slave revolt

60
Pompey, Crassus, and Julius Caesar form First Triumvirate

58–50
Caesar conquers Gaul

48–44
Caesar defeats Pompey and rules as dictator

44
Caesar is assassinated on Ides of March

44–31
Marc Antony, Lepidus (until 36), and Octavian rule as Second Triumvirate

40–4
Herod rules as King of Judaea

31
Octavian defeats Antony and Cleopatra at Actium

30
Marc Antony and Cleopatra die; Octavian becomes sole ruler of Roman world

27 BCE–476 CE
The Roman Empire

27 BCE–14 CE
Octavian takes name of Augustus and rules for 40 years; Golden age of Latin literature: Virgil, Horace, and Livy write

13
Augustus builds the Ara Pacis (Altar of Peace)

4
Jesus of Nazareth is born

CE

9
Varus is defeated by German leader Arminius

14–37
Reign of Tiberius

37–41
Reign of Caligula

41–54
Reign of Claudius

43
Claudius conquers Britain

54–68
Reign of Nero

64
Fire destroys much of Rome

68–69
Civil War of the Four Emperors

69–79
Reign of Vespasian; Titus captures Jerusalem

79–81
Reign of Titus

79
Mt. Vesuvius erupts and destroys Pompeii

80
Titus opens Colosseum

81–96
Reign of Domitian

96–180
Tacitus, Pliny, Suetonius, and Juvenal write, at the height of the Silver age of Latin literature

98–117
Reign of Trajan; Trajan conquers Dacia

117–138
Reign of Hadrian

126
Hadrian's Wall completed in Britain

161–180
Reign of Marcus Aurelius

235–284
Chaos in Rome; 50 emperors rule, one after another

250–251
Christians all over the empire are arrested, and many are killed

284–305
Reign of Diocletian

285
Diocletian divides empire into East and West; forms rule of four

303
Diocletian orders persecution of Christians

312–476
The Christian Empire

306–337
Reign of Constantine

312
Constantine conquers Rome

313
Constantine legalizes Christianity

330
Constantine founds Constantinople

379–395
Reign of Theodosius; Theodosius outlaws paganism

395
Permanent division of the empire

395–1453
Byzantine Empire

410
Goths sack Rome

453
Attila the Hun approaches gates of Rome

476
Rome falls to invading Goths; German king Odoacer rules Rome

527–565
Reign of Justinian

FURTHER READING

Entries with “ indicate primary source material.

GENERAL WORKS ON ANCIENT ROME

Boardman, John, ed. *The Oxford History of the Roman World.* New York: Oxford University Press, 2001.

Brown, Peter. *The World of Late Antiquity.* New York: Thames & Hudson, 1971.

Cameron, Averil. *The Later Roman Empire.* Cambridge, Mass.: Harvard University Press, 1993.

Connolly, Peter, and Hazel Dodge. *The Ancient City: Life in Classical Athens and Rome.* New York: Oxford University Press, 1998.

“ De Selincourt, Aubrey, trans. *Livy: The Early History of Rome,* bks 1–5. New York: Penguin, 2002.

Drinkwater, J. F., and Andrew Drummond. *The World of the Romans.* New York: Oxford, 1993.

Langley, Andrew. *The Roman News.* Cambridge, Mass.: Candlewick Press, 1999.

“ Lewis, Naphtali and Meyer Reinhold. *Roman Civilization*, 3rd ed. New York: Columbia University Press, 1990.

Lintott, Andrew. *The Roman Republic.* Stroud, England: Sutton Publishing, 2001.

Nardo, Don. *The Age of Augustus.* San Diego, Calif.: Lucent, 1997.

——. *The Decline and Fall of the Roman Empire.* San Diego, Calif.: Lucent, 1998.

Scarre, Christopher. *Chronicle of the Roman Emperors: The Reign-by-Reign Record of the Rulers of Imperial Rome.* New York: Thames & Hudson, 1995.

“ Shelton, Jo-Ann. *As the Romans Did*, 2nd ed. New York: Oxford University Press, 1998.

Solway, Andrew. *Rome: In Spectacular Cross-Section.* New York: Scholastic, 2003.

Solway, Andrew, and Peter Connolly. *Ancient Rome.* New York: Oxford University Press, 2001.

Tingay, Graham, and Anthony Marks. *The Romans.* Newton, Mass.: EDC Publications, 1991.

Wells, C. M. *The Roman Empire.* Cambridge, Mass.: Harvard University Press, 1995.

ATLASES

Haywood, John. *World Atlas of the Past, vol. 1: The Ancient World.* New York: Oxford University Press, 1999.

——. *Penguin Historical Atlas of Ancient Rome.* New York: Penguin, 1995.

DICTIONARIES AND ENCYCLOPEDIAS

Adkins, Roy and Leslie. *Handbook to Life in Ancient Rome.* New York: Oxford University Press, 1998.

Moulton, Carroll, ed. *Ancient Greece and Rome: An Encyclopedia for Students.* New York: Scribner, 1998.

BIOGRAPHY

Baker, Rosalie, and Charles Baker. *Ancient Romans: Expanding the Classical Tradition.* New York: Oxford University Press, 1998.

Forsyth, Fiona. *Augustus: The First Emperor.* New York: Rosen, 2003.

“ Graves, Robert, trans. *Suetonius: The Twelve Caesars.* New York: Penguin, 2003.

Scott-Kilvert, Ian, trans. *Plutarch: Makers of Rome: Coriolanus, Fabius Maximus, Macellus, Cato the Elder, Tiberius Gracchus, Gaius Gracchus, Sertorius, Brutus, Mark Antony.* New York: Penguin, 1965.

Southern, Pat. *Augustus.* New York: Routledge, 1998.

Stockton, David. *Cicero: A Political Biography.* New York: Oxford University Press, 1971.

——. *The Gracchi.* New York: Oxford University Press, 1979.

Warner, Rex, trans. *Plutarch: Fall of the Roman Republic: Marius, Sulla, Crassus, Pompey, Caesar, Cicero.* New York: Penguin, 1959.

ART AND ARCHITECTURE

D'Ambra, Eve. *Roman Art.* New York: Cambridge University Press, 1998.

Grant, Michael. *Art in the Roman Empire.* New York: Routledge, 1995.

GLADIATORS

Potter, D. S., and D. J. Mattingly. *Life, Death, and Entertainment in the Roman Empire.* Ann Arbor: University of Michigan Press, 1999.

Watkins, Richard. *Gladiator.* Boston: Houghton Mifflin, 2000.

MILITARY

Connolly, Peter. *The Legionary.* New York: Oxford University Press, 1998.

——. *The Roman Fort.* New York: Oxford University Press, 1998.

Gabriel, Richard A. *The Great Armies of Antiquity.* Westport, Conn.: Praeger, 2002.

Nardo, Don. *Life of a Roman Soldier.* San Diego, Calif.: Lucent, 2000.

Platt, Richard. *Julius Caesar.* New York: DK Publishing, 2001.

POMPEII

Coarelli, Filippo, ed. *Pompeii.* New York: Riverside, 2002.

Connolly, Peter. *Pompeii.* New York: Oxford University Press, 1990.

Grant, Michael. *Cities of Vesuvius: Pompeii & Herculaneum.* New York: Penguin, 1976.

RELIGION

Beard, Mary, John North, and Simon Price. *Religions of Rome: Volume 2, A Sourcebook.* New York: Cambridge University Press, 1998.

Chadwick, Henry. *The Early Church.* New York: Penguin, 1993.

SCIENCE AND TECHNOLOGY

Hamey, L. A., and J. A. Hamey. *The Roman Engineers.* New York: Cambridge University Press, 1981.

Harris, Jacqueline. *Science in Ancient Rome.* New York: Watts, 1998.

WOMEN

Fantham, Elaine., et al. *Women in the Classical World.* New York: Oxford University Press, 1994.

MacDonald, Fiona. *Cleopatra.* New York: DK Publishing, 2001.

——. *Women in Ancient Rome.* Lincolnwood, Ill.: Peter Bedrick, 2000.

Nardo, Don. *Women of Ancient Rome.* San Diego, Calif.: Lucent, 2003.

WEBSITES

GATEWAYS

About.com Ancient/Classical History
http://ancienthistory.about.com/cs/rome/
Provides extensive links to websites and materials on ancient Rome; includes reviews of television programs on Rome and access to on-line discussions.

Audio-Visual Resources For Classics
http://lilt.ilstu.edu/drjclassics2/Files/romangeneral.shtm
This section of Dr. Janice Siegel's *Illustrated Guide to the Classical World* points users to videos, CD-ROMs, and video games.

Bill Thayer's Roman Sites
http://penelope.uchicago.edu/Thayer/E/home.html
Links to more than 2,300 websites dealing with various aspects of ancient Rome.

Internet Ancient History Sourcebook
www.fordham.edu/halsall/ancient/asbook09.html
Complete texts (Livy, Suetonius, and more) and thematically arranged selections on topics such as Roman slavery.

The Perseus Digital Library
www.perseus.tufts.edu
Works of classical literature and images of classical art; more is available on CD-ROM.

WEBSITES

The British Museum
www.thebritishmuseum.ac.uk/world/rome/rome.html
Images of hundreds of British Museum objects with detailed descriptions—particularly good for coinage, Roman Britain, and sculpture.

Daily Life in Ancient Rome
http://members.aol.com/Donnclass/Romelife.html
Material about topics such as Roman weddings, school, and clothing.

Feminae Romanae: The Women of Ancient Rome
http://dominae.fws1.com/
Detailed explanations and images of the experiences of Roman women.

Illustrated History of the Roman Empire
www.roman-empire.net
Historical and visual material, including interactive maps, timelines, and links.

The Internet Classics Archive
http://classics.mit.edu/
Provides access to more than 400 works of classical literature by 59 authors.

The Roman Empire
www.pbs.org/empires/romans
Based on the public television series, *The Roman Empire*, the site includes an extensive timeline, games, and a family tree.

The Romans
www.bbc.co.uk/schools/romans
This exciting site includes weblinks, interactive sites, games, and material from many BBC series. It is primarily concerned with the Romans in Britain.

Smith's Smaller Classical Dictionary
www.classicaldictionary.bravepages.com/
An easy-to-use, 460-page on-line dictionary of people and places.

INDEX

References to illustrations and their captions are indicated by page numbers in **bold**.

TEXT CREDITS

All texts, except where noted, have been translated or adapted from Latin or Greek by the authors.

ABBREVIATIONS

Caesars: Robert Graves, trans. *Suetonius: The Twelve Caesars,* New York: Penguin, 2003.

Makers: Ian Scott-Kilvert, trans. *Plutarch: Makers of Rome, Nine Lives,* New York: Penguin, 1965.

Roman Civilization: Naphtali Lewis and Meyer Reinhold, *Roman Civilization,* vol. 2, 3rd ed. New York: Columbia University Press, 1990.

Shelton: Jo-Ann Shelton, *As the Romans Did,* 2nd ed. New York: Oxford University Press, 1998.

CIL: *Corpus Inscriptionum Latinarum* (in Latin).

ILS: *Inscriptiones Latinae Selectae* (in Latin).

MAIN TEXT

p. 14: Virgil, *The Aeneid,* bk. 1, lines 1–7.

p. 15: Dionysius of Halicarnassus, *Roman Antiquities,* bk. 1, ch. 72.

p. 16: Livy, *From the Founding of the City,* bk., 1 ch. 4.

p. 20: Herodotus, *Histories,* bk. 1, ch. 94.

p. 21: Dionysius of Halicarnassus, *Roman Antiquities,* bk. 1, ch. 30, para. 1–3.

p. 26: Livy, *From the Founding of the City,* bk. 1, ch. 58–9.

p. 30: Livy, *From the Founding of the City,* bk. 2, ch. 10.

p. 31: Livy, *From the Founding of the City,* bk. 3, ch. 26.

p. 33: Livy, *From the Founding of the City,* bk. 2, ch. 32.

p. 35: Euripides, *Suppliants,* lines 433–4.

p. 36: E. H. Warmington, ed. and trans., *Remains of Old Latin*, vol. 4 (London: Heinemann, 1940) no. 10.

p. 36: E. H. Warmington, ed. and trans., *Remains of Old Latin*, vol. 4 (London: Heinemann, 1940) no. 2.

p. 38: Aulus Gellius, *Attic Nights,* bk. 1, ch. 12, para. 1–2, 6, 9, 14.

p. 40: Livy, *From the Founding of the City,* bk. 5, ch. 21.

p. 41: Livy, *From the Founding of the City,* bk. 21, ch. 1.

p. 41: Livy, *From the Founding of the City,* bk. 21, ch. 1.

p. 47: Plutarch, *Life of Cato,* ch. 27.

p. 47: Plutarch, *Life of Cato,* ch. 20.

p. 48: Plutarch, *Life of Cato,* ch. 4.

p. 51: Plutarch, *Life of Cato,* ch. 12.

p. 52: Cicero, *About Constitutions,* bk. 3, ch. 3, para. 6–9.

p. 52: Plutarch, *Life of Cato,* ch. 23 (trans. in *Makers,* p. 146).

p. 54: *ILS* 8731 (trans. in *Shelton,* p. 177 no. 215)

p. 54: Diodorus Siculus, *History of the World,* bk. 5, ch. 38, para. 1. (trans. in *Shelton,* p. 172 no. 209)

p. 55: Cato, *On Agriculture,* bk. 2, ch. 56.

p. 55: Plutarch, *Life of Crassus,* ch. 8.

p. 57: Plutarch, *Life of Crassus,* ch. 10.

p. 59: Plutarch, *Life of Tiberius Gracchus,* ch. 2.

p. 61: Sallust, *Catiline,* ch. 10.

p. 61: Plutarch, *Life of Tiberius Gracchus,* ch. 9.

p. 66: Appian, *Civil Wars,* bk. 2, ch. 7.

p. 66: Cicero, *Letters to Atticus*, bk. 12, letter 15 (trans. in *Shelton*, p. 92 no. 124).

p. 67: Cicero, *Essay on Duties*, bk. 1, ch. 42 (trans. in *Shelton*, p. 126 no. 163).

p. 68: Cicero, *On the Manilian Law,* 22, 65.

p. 70: Cicero, *Letters to his Friends*, bk. 5, letter 7.

p. 71: Cicero, *Second Philippic,* ch. 46 para. 117.

p. 71: Plutarch, *Life of Cicero,* ch. 49.

p. 73: Plutarch, *Life of Caesar,* ch. 63.

p. 74: Suetonius, *Life of the Deified Julius,* ch. 22.

p. 76: Plutarch, *Life of Caesar,* ch. 46.

p. 76: Plutarch, *Life of Caesar,* ch. 50.

p. 78: Suetonius, *Life of the Deified Julius,* ch. 82.

p. 80: Plutarch, *Life of Antony,* ch. 27 (trans. in *Makers*, p. 294).

p. 82: Plutarch, *Life of Antony,* ch. 26 (trans. in *Makers*, p. 293).

p. 82: Plutarch, *Life of Antony,* ch. 29 (trans. in *Makers*, p. 296).

p. 85: Plutarch, *Life of Antony,* ch. 76 (trans. in *Makers*, p. 340).

p. 85: Plutarch, *Life of Antony,* ch. 77 (trans. in *Makers*, p. 341).

p. 86: Plutarch, *Life of Antony,* ch. 86 (trans. in *Makers*, p. 348).

p. 87: Augustus, *My Achievements*, ch. 1.

p. 90: Augustus, *My Achievements*, ch. 34.

p. 91: Suetonius, *Life of Augustus*, ch. 28.

p. 93: Suetonius, *Life of Augustus*, ch. 99.

p. 93: Augustus, *My Achievements*, ch. 35.

p. 94: Suetonius, *Life of Claudius*, ch. 4 (trans. in *Caesars*, pp. 183–4).

p. 96: Suetonius, *Life of Tiberius*, ch. 68 (trans. in *Caesars*, p. 143).

p. 97: Suetonius, *Life of Caligula*, ch. 22 (trans. in *Caesars*, p. 159).

p. 100: Suetonius, *Life of Nero*, ch. 49.

p. 101: Suetonius, *Life of Vespasian,* ch. 15 (trans. in *Caesars*, p. 282).

p. 101: Suetonius, *Life of Vespasian,* ch. 23.

p. 101: Tacitus, *Life of Agricola*, ch. 45.

p. 102: Pliny the Younger, *Letters*, bk. 4, letter 19 (trans. in *Shelton*, p. 45 no. 61).

p. 102: *ILS*, 8158 (trans. in *Shelton*, p. 46 no. 64).

p. 103: Valerius Maximus, *Memorable Deeds and Words*, bk. 6, ch. 3, para. 9 (trans. in *Shelton*, p. 47 no. 66).

p. 103: Catullus, *Poems*, 61, lines 57–62.

p. 104: *ILS* 7691 (trans. in *Shelton*, p. 112 no. 51).

p. 105: Horace, *Epistles*, bk. 2, poem 1, line 70.

p. 105: Suetonius, *A Book about Schoolteachers*, 9 (trans. in *Shelton*, p. 103 no. 137).

p. 105: Juvenal, *Satires*, ch. 6.

p. 108: Pliny the Younger, *Letters*, bk. 6, letter 16.

p. 109: Pliny the Younger, *Letters*, bk. 6, letter 16.

p. 110: Pliny the Younger, *Letters*, bk. 6, letter 16.

p. 110: Pliny, *Natural History*, bk. 20, ch. 260–01.

p. 111: Pliny the Younger, *Letters*, bk. 6, letter 20.

p. 111: Pliny the Younger, *Letters*, bk. 6, letter 20.

p. 113: *CIL*, vol. 4 no. 429 (trans. in *Shelton*, p. 220 no. 263); 1477; 4948 (trans. in *Shelton*, p. 327 no. 371); 9123 (trans. in *Shelton*, p. 99 no. 132).

p. 114: *Année Epigraphique* 1969–70 no. 583 (trans. in *Roman Civilization,* p. 494 no. 152).

p. 116: Josephus, *The Jewish War,* bk. 3, ch. 71 (trans. in *Shelton,* p. 253 no. 294).

p. 116: Cassius Dio, *Roman History,* bk. 49, ch. 30.

p. 118: Pliny the Younger, *Panegyricus,* 65.

p. 119: *CIL,* vol. 16 no. 48.

p. 121: Martial, *On the Games,* ch. 26.

p. 122: Fronto, *Elements of History,* ch. 18.

p. 124: Sidonius Apollinaris, *Poems,* ch. 23 (trans. in *Shelton,* p. 339 no. 381).

p. 125: *ILS* 5287 (trans. in *Shelton,* p. 342 no. 384).

p. 126: *CIL* vol. 4 no. 4397 & 4356 (trans. in *Shelton,* p. 352 no. 394).

p. 127: Seneca the Younger, *Letters,* bk. 7, letter 2 (trans. in *Shelton,* p. 355 no. 398).

p. 128: *CIL,* vol. 10, no. 810.

p. 128: *CIL,* vol. 10, no. 811.

p. 130: Andrew Slayman, "Sunken Ships of Pisa," *Archaeology,* no. 3 (May-June, 1999); "A Cache of Vintage Ships," *Archaeology* no. 3 (July-August, 1999).

p. 130: David Keys, "Archaeologists Hunt for a Roman Troop Ship," *The Independent* (London), 19 April 2001.

p. 131: David Keys, "Roman aqueduct 280 miles long uncovered in Turkish forest," *The Independent* (London), 22 July 2001.

p. 132: Aelius Aristeides, *In Praise of Rome,* 200–01 (trans. in *Shelton,* p. 136, no. 172).

p. 133: *Augustan History, Life of Hadrian,* ch. 1.

p. 134: *Augustan History, Life of Hadrian,* ch. 13.

p. 134: *Augustan History, Life of Hadrian,* ch. 16 (trans. A. Birley, *Cambridge Ancient History,* vol. 11, New York: Cambridge University Press, 2000, p. 138).

p. 134: *Augustan History, Life of Hadrian,* ch. 17.

p. 136: ILS 9134 (trans. in *Roman Civilization,* vol. 2 p. 462).

p. 138: Pliny the Elder, *Natural History,* bk. 28, ch. 5, para. 23–9 (trans. in *Shelton,* p. 418. no. 455).

p. 138: Seneca the Younger, *On Mercy,* 2, 5, 1.

p. 139: *ILS,* 8753 (trans. in *Shelton,* p. 344 no. 385).

p. 140: Cato, *On Agriculture,* 160 (trans. in *Shelton,* p. 419 no. 456).

p. 141: Suetonius, *Life of Augustus,* ch. 100.

p. 141: Suetonius, *Life of Vespasian,* ch. 23.

p. 142: Livy, *From the Founding of the City,* bk. 29, ch. 14.

p. 144: Tacitus, *The Life of Agricola,* ch. 30.

p. 144: Tacitus, *Histories,* bk. 4, para. 74.

p. 146: Synesius, *Letters,* ch. 148.

p. 146: The Gospel According to Luke 2:1, 3–4.

p. 150: The Bk. of Genesis 2:1–2.

p. 151: The Bk. of Exodus 20:3.

p. 152: First Bk. of Maccabees 5:47–50, 56.

p. 153: First Bk. of Maccabees 8:19–20.

p. 153: The Gospel According to Matthew 2:1–2.

p. 155: The Gospel According to Luke 2:24.

p. 155: The Gospel According to Luke 2:30, 32*b*.

p. 155: The Bk. of Isaiah 42:1, 4.

p. 155: The Bk. of Zechariah 9:9.

p. 155: The Bk. of Micah 5:2.

p. 157: The Gospel According to Matthew 5:3–10.

p. 157: The Gospel According to Matthew 22: 21.

p. 157: The Gospel According to Matthew 5:38–9.

p. 157: The Gospel According to Luke 10:27, 29.

p. 159: Tacitus, *Annals,* bk. 15, ch. 44 (trans. in *Shelton,* p. 409 no. 446).

p. 160: Eusebius, *Ecclesiastical History,* 28.

p. 163: Tacitus, *The Annals,* bk. 1, ch. 61.

p. 163: Suetonius, *Life of Augustus,* 23.

p. 167: Lactantius, *Divine Institutes,* bk. 7, ch. 25 (trans. in *Roman Civilization,* p. 628).

p. 167: Anonymous, *The Life of Leo the Great,* (trans. in J. H. Robinson, *Readings in European History,* Boston: Ginn, 1905, pp. 49–51).

p. 168: Symmachus, *Dispatches to the Emperor,* 3:8–10 (trans. in *Shelton,* p. 391 no. 433).

p. 172: Peter Brown, *The World of Late Antiquity*. New York: Norton, 1989, p. 123.

p. 175: Cicero, *On Duties,* bk. 1, section 34.

SIDEBARS

p. 46: Polybius, *Histories,* bk. 39, ch. 5.

p. 68: Cicero, *On the Orator,* bk. 1, para. 16–20 (trans. in *Shelton* p. 119 no. 159).

p. 136: A. K. Bowman, *Life and Letters on the Roman Frontier*. New York: Routledge, 1998.

PICTURE CREDITS

Alinari/ Art Resource, NY: 27, 47, 68, 107, 131; By courtesy of APT - Rome: 121, 169; Brooklyn Museum of Art: 82; © Maureen A. Burns: 128; Colchester Museums: 105; Pseudo-Cicerp Rhetorica ad Herennium, Italy, mid 14th century. Misc. Bd. Ms. 145. Division of Rare Books and Manuscript Collections, Cornell University Library: 67; Werner Forman/Art Resource, NY: 40, 103, 112; FOTOTECA UNIONE: 25, 90, 138; J. Paul Getty Museum, Malibu, California: 142, Gift of Achille Moretti 57; Giraudon/Art Resource, NY: 34, 64, 100; © 1998 Itamar Grinberg, "Courtesy of the Israel Ministry of Tourism": 154; Netherlandish, anonymous, after Cornelius Cort, The Battle of Zama, c.1750, oil on panel, 42.7x59cm, George F. Harding Collection, 1990.563: 46; HIP/Scala/Art Resource, NY: 114, 143, 147; Albert Hoxie Photo Archives, UCLA: 30, 75, 117, 119, 126, 137, 146, 148, 166, 170, 171; Courtesy of the Israel Ministry of Tourism: 151; Erich Lessing / Art Resource, NY: 2, 11, 35, 48, 94, 98, 106, 133, 145, 150; Courtesy of Los Angeles Memorial Coliseum Commission: 176; Gilles Mermet/Art Resource, NY: 32, 58; "The Metropolitan Museum of Art , Purchase, Joseph Pulitzer Bequest, 1955 (55.121.5) Photograph © 1992 The Metropolitan Museum of Art": 81; "The Metropolitan Museum of Art, Harris Brisbane Dick Fund, 1940 (40.11.7-.18) Photograph © 1983 The Metropolitan Museum of Art": 22; "The Metropolitan Museum of Art, Harris Brisbane Dick Fund, 1946 (46.160) Photograph © 1992 The Metropolitan Museum of Art": 18; "The Metropolitan Museum of Art, Rogers Fund, 1903 (03.14.13a-g) Photograph © 1986 The Metropolitan Museum of Art": 49; University of Michigan Museum of Art; Museum Purchase 1953/1.47: 172; Réunion des Musées Nationaux/ AR: 123; © National Maritime Museum, London: 84; Nimatallah/Art Resouce, NY: 10, 89; Courtesy of Photofest: 53, 83; Réunion des Musées Nationaux/Art Resource, NY: 24, 41, 97, 123; Scala/Art Resource, NY: 11, 14, 21,29, 36, 39, 44, 45, 51, 55, 59, 71, 73, 87, 113, 120, 129, 140, 149, 158, 160, 163, 167; SEF/Art Resource, NY: 135; Ronald Sheridan, Ancient Art & Architecture Collection: 72; Smithsonian American Art Museum, Washington, DC/Art Resource, NY: 173; Staatliche Museen zu Berlin-PreuBischer Kulturbesitz, Antikensammlung (Johannes Laurentis)/ bpk 2003: 79; Photo by Jim Steinhart of www.planetware.com: 19, 162, 175; Vroma project, www.vroma.org: 122; The Walters Art Museum, Baltimore: 77; © Yale Center for British Art, Paul Mellon Collection, USA/Photo: Bridgeman Art Library: 109.

ACKNOWLEDGMENTS

We would like to thank our editors Nancy Toff, Karen Fein, and Nancy Hirsch for their patience and wisdom; our friend and colleague Amanda Podany for her sense of balance and good humor; and the scholars, teachers, and middle-school students who have helped us to shape this book.

MARNI MCGEE was born in New Orleans and grew up in Charlotte, North Carolina. Her love of words began in childhood. She remembers sitting around the dinner table at night with her father, mother, older sister, and younger brother—all talking about the day. Along with the fried chicken and grits were dishes of laughter, teasing, memories, and stories. Many of her books spring from these family experiences. She began writing children's books in 1974 and has been a full-time writer since 1994. Her work—published in the United States, United Kingdom, and Korea—includes award-winning picture books, easy readers, poetry, and historical fiction. She is an avid traveler with a special love for England and Italy. Her "favorite things" include beach walks, reading, theater, and music, especially chamber music and opera. McGee lives with her husband in Santa Barbara, California, and is the mother of two grown children.

RONALD MELLOR, who is professor of history at UCLA, first became enthralled with ancient history as a student at Regis High School in New York City. He is the statewide faculty advisor of the California History–Social Science Project (CHSSP), which brings university faculty together with K-12 teachers at sites throughout California. In 2000, the American Historical Association awarded the CHSSP the Albert J. Beveridge Award for K-12 teaching. Professor Mellor has held fellowships from the National Endowment for the Humanities and the American Council of Learned Societies. His research has centered on ancient religion and Roman historiography. His books include *Theia Rhome: The Goddess Roma in the Greek World* (1975), *From Augustus to Nero: The First Dynasty of Imperial Rome* (1990), *Tacitus* (1993), *Tacitus: The Classical Heritage* (1995), *The Historians of Ancient Rome* (1997), and *The Roman Historians* (2nd edition, 2004).

AMANDA PODANY is a specialist in the history of the ancient Near East and a professor of history at California State Polytechnic University, Pomona. She has taught there since 1990 and is currently serving as the director of the university's honors program. From 1993 to 1997 she was executive director of the California History–Social Science Project, a professional development program for history–social science teachers at all grade levels. Her work in professional development for teachers has received major grants from the California Postsecondary Education Commission and the United States Department of Education. Her publications include *The Land of Hana: Kings, Chronology, and Scribal Tradition*. Professor Podany has also published numerous journal articles on ancient Near Eastern history and on approaches to teaching. She is co-author of *The Ancient Near Eastern World* in the World in Ancient Times series. She lives in Los Angeles with her husband and two children.